All That Appears
Isn't Necessarily So:
Morality, Virtue,
Politics, and Education

By Robert P. Engvall

1

All That Appears Isn't Necessarily So: Morality, Virtue, Politics, and Education

By Robert P. Engvall

Copyright 1998 by Robert P. Engvall

Published by Caddo Gap Press
   3145 Geary Boulevard, Suite 275
   San Francisco, California 94118 U.S.A.

ISBN 1-880192-26-8

Price $19.95 U.S.

Library of Congress Cataloging-in-Publication Data

Engvall, Robert P.
   All that appears isn't necessarily so : morality, virtue,
politics, and education / by Robert P. Engvall.
      p.   cm.
   Includes bibliographical references (p.) and index.
   ISBN 1-880192-26-8 (alk. paper)
   1. Politics and education--United States. 2. Moral education-
-United States. 3. Virtue. 4. Education--Social aspects--United
States.   I. Title.
LC89.E54 1998
379.73--dc21   98-7095
                                                      CIP

Contents

3

Preface

In recent years, the frequency of social critics' attacks upon our collective "loss of virtue" have heightened. These attacks have centered upon our collective "failures" within various social structures. Concerns have been continually raised about our schools, our political foundations, and most recently, and no doubt most painfully, about ourselves. Such attacks on our "failures" now occur so routinely that we often treat the message as so obvious that it need only be mentioned to be accepted. This book attacks that message, not so much for its content, as for its method of delivery. In other words, I'm setting out to attack not the message, but the messenger. I might attempt to attack the message as well, but for the fact that the message is far too complicated for a person like myself to understand. "Virtue" is, after all, rather complicated.

Unfortunately in our "quick fix" society, we have been led to believe that merely following the advice of others or adhering to "virtues" as set forth in fairy tales and anecdotes will allow all of us to live in perfect harmony. Similarly, failure to adhere to the "advice" as suggested by the "self-proclaimed experts of virtue" will accordingly lead us straight down the road to ruin—if not hell. While it is not my desire to burn in hell any more than most, it is troubling to me to think that following the words of William Bennett and/or Rush Limbaugh might improve my chances for a more temperate climate after death. In fact, as I hope this work addresses, following the words of persons like those might actually increase my chances of meeting eternal damnation, or at least improve my chances of listening to Limbaugh on radio and/or buying the collective works of Bennett, either of which could be easily misinterpreted as actually suffering in hell.

But Enough About Me...

Even if we accept the premise of our collective societal failure as true, the issue beyond lamenting our status becomes the more practical one of what might we do to correct this fall from grace. This work focuses upon how sadly misguided we have become (which may or may not support the thesis that we have lost our virtue) in the way that we so blindly accept what the "experts" on virtue tell us. If we have fallen, we will not get up through a careful adherence to the "virtues" presented in recent best-sellers. It is, sadly, more difficult than that. Contrary to much popular belief, virtue is not a "thing" that we have lost or misplaced. It is, therefore, more difficult to find than one's keys, or one's television remote control. Virtue is instead a journey, a continuing struggle, and hopefully perhaps a calling. A calling that should seldom be associated with the actual persons most successful at attacking the virtues of the rest of us while they ably proclaim their own.

A recent *Phi Delta Kappa / Gallup Poll* (1996) concerning our public schools tends to support our concerns over our "loss." Among its findings, "good citizenship" becomes the most frequently cited "purpose of the public schools" among respondents who were given a list of potential purposes. Since evidence of the legitimacy and/or frequency of the problem is growing and our concern about the problem grows accordingly, we tend to be more susceptible to, and less critical of, remedies that might have little more value than the "tonics" and "cure-alls" sold from the back of wagons in bygone eras.

That we societally have lost something, or perhaps a sign that the apocalypse really is upon us, can easily be imagined with no more effort than a look into the windows of a bookstore. Rather than novels by John Steinbeck, Kurt Vonnegut, E.L. Doctorow, Ernest Hemingway, and countless other writers, we have works by such literary luminaries as Marcia Clark, Dennis Rodman, and Howard Stern. It is abundantly clear that we have indeed seen a transformation. This work argues, however, that it is less a transformation through a lessening of our collective "virtue" than it is a lessening of our collective intellectual capacities, which in turn makes us ripe for the kind of "blather" that we have come to expect to receive via television, but which we now unfortunately receive endlessly in print as well. The publishers cannot be blamed, at least entirely, as our free market society amply rewards those who publish the works of Rodman and Stern far more than it does those attempting to publish more "scholarly" works. To paraphrase our new American icon (and best-selling author) Rodman, it's more than a societal acceptance of "As Bad As I Wanna Be"—it's in fact a widespread societal conspiracy, practiced both knowingly and unknowingly by millions of Americans, the title of which might read "As Bad As We Allow It to Be."

Introduction

Ideology...is an instrument of power; a defense mechanism against information; a pretext for eluding moral constraints in doing or approving evil with a clean conscience; and finally, a way of banning the criterion of experience, that is, of completely eliminating or indefinitely postponing the pragmatic criteria of success and failure.

—Jean-Francois Revel

Beware...of windbags and pious souls who presume to know what is moral for you and your family. (Katz, 1997, p. xxv)

In today's increasingly complex and multi-cultural world, and amid the American political climate of growing intolerance and widening polarity, there exists a real and present danger that threatens to underlie American social policy generally and educational policy specifically. This danger lies in the ever-expanding sphere of influence that many persons have acquired, despite lacking facts to support their views. Barbara J. Duncan (1997) writes: "...after the Reagan 'go-go' '80s, an era of fast profits, quick deals, and increased emphasis on individual problems and solutions, many Americans feel as if something is now missing from society" (p. 119). Witness the recent call to "volunteerism." The yawning gap between the rhetoric about helping the needy and the reality of mean-spirited public policy and budget cuts was "filled" by our proclamations about the great American tradition of volunteerism.

Among the most troublesome aspects of this "call to virtue," as it is often proclaimed, is that many of those most heard in their cries lamenting our present societal condition are the same persons who were at the forefront proclaiming the "virtue" of those "go-go" 80s. If the world has truly "gone to hell in a handbasket" as many would have us believe, it seems peculiar that we seek to be reshaped or even reborn under the guidance of those very same people who played a hand in leading us there. Meg Greenfield (1997) wrote of her fascination with our society's ability to grant "standing" to persons who seem to lack such authority. In her words, "standing to be listened to, or to be taken seriously on a subject" has been granted with too much frequency to too many. In my words, "I agree."

A great danger facing all of us, and particularly our youth, is less a loss of virtue than the belief on the part of some that youth need to follow one path to virtue and/or that "their virtues" are those that should be inculcated. The influence these "primers," particularly the most "virtuous" among them, and the value that the elixers they promote have upon social and educational policy is the centerpiece of this book.

> Vision has become self-contained and self-justifying—which is to say, independent of empirical evidence. That is what makes it dangerous, not because a particular set of policies may be flawed or counterproductive, but because insulation from evidence virtually guarantees a never-ending supply of policies and practices fatally independent of reality. Moreover, the pervasiveness of the vision of the annointed at all levels of the American educational system ensures future supplies of people indoctrinated with this vision and also convinced that they

10

should "make a difference"—that public policy-making is to be seen as ego gratification from imposing one's vision on other people through the power of government. (Sowell, 1995, p. 241)

The annointed claim to share our society's "collective" vision of morality. When "annointed" is used pejoratively it refers to those "favored persons" frequenting the other side of the political spectrum, whichever side that happens to be. Our collective abilities to view ourselves as marginalized, while we simultaneously view our positions on social issues as "mainstream" is, and should be, a wonderment to us all. The "annointed" to Thomas Sowell seems to consist of "liberals" whose positions are propigated, in Sowell's view, without challenge. The "annointed" to me are persons like William Bennett and Rush Limbaugh, whose words are given far too much credibility, and challenged far too little, when indeed they are challenged at all. If we cannot even agree upon who are the "annointed" it will be dauntingly difficult to agree upon whose virtues should rule.

Perhaps even more important than whose "virtues" we might adhere to, is the rigid viewpoint that either the "right" or the "left" has sole control of the concept of virtue. Christopher Lasch (1995) laments his belief that both "left and right-wing ideologies are now so rigid that new ideas make little impression on their adherents" (p. 80). "The faithful," or "true believers" as Eric Hoffer would have referred to them, "have sealed themselves off from arguments and events that might call their own convictions into question" (pp. 80-81). Sealing themselves off from debate allows for the type of "candid conversation" that Limbaugh allows only those with his perspective. Al Franken's satirical and very popular work spoke of Limbaugh's radio show "screening" callers to make certain that all who receive airtime share the views of Limbaugh. Debate in such a venue is not only discouraged, it is entirely forbidden. Lasch writes: "Instead of engaging unfamiliar arguments, they are content to classify them as either orthodox or heretical" (p. 81). This description quite ably defines Limbaugh and others like him who portray those who disagree as "femi-nazis, environmentalist whackos," and the like. Before *The Book of Virtues* was released, James Q. Wilson (1993) foretold of the future in which political actors would exploit our loss of virtue (real and imagined) for political and personal gain. That future is here and now, and is not solely the province of Bennett, although he may be our best symbol of one who speaks for all of us (at least in his mind) when it comes to virtue. The trouble for some, myself included, lies in our abdication of the "virtuous highground" to someone like Bennett, who seems less a paragon of virtue than a paragon of divisiveness, competitiveness, and outright greed. Greenfield writes that those who best illustrate standing "never realize that there is a problem" (p. 86). If character really does count, as Bennett and others preached that it should during their campaign for Bob Dole's presidential candidacy in 1996, maybe our society's vision of character includes a wider cross-section of persons than those Bennett would care to admit to the virtuous highground. Rather than assume that character didn't count since their "character filled" man was defeated and another "character flawed" man was elected, perhaps they missed the point of what the concept of character was and remains all about. Perhaps the politics of "hope" and inclusiveness shows more "character" and more "virtue" than do the politics of divisiveness.

"Moral understanding and action depend on vision; vision depends on character; character must be shaped by those who come before us. But what justifies their claim to a vision of moral truth? By whom was their character shaped?" (Meilaender, 1984, p. 99). For whatever faults Bill Clinton brought and brings forth, perhaps the "character" of those who opposed him was equally as suspect. Most importantly, perhaps their claims to the appropriate vision of "moral truth" are shaky at best.

The debate over whether "virtue can and should be taught?" is not new. Scholars, both contemporary and ancient, have considered the question. It was, in fact, the subject of Plato's *Protagoras*. Socrates himself expressed doubt that virtue could be taught (Meilaender, 1984). Our experience likewise "suggests that virtue cannot be taught" (Meilaender, 1984, p. 49). Of course G.C. Meilaender's book *The Theory and Practice of Virtue*, an academic discourse on the philosophy of virtue, sold hundreds of thousands less than did Bennett's *The Book of Virtues*. It seems, in our age of supermarkets (in the macroeconomic sense) and superconsumers, simple how-to lists are much more pleasurable than thoughtful treatises. Bennett's how-to lists seem to compare favorably to his former role as Secretary of Education, in which he oversaw top-down mandates and pleas for curricular and instructional uniformity; conformity to "his ways," as often the "only ways" if not the "virtuous ways." Conformity does not always illustrate character or virtue, certainly southerners who conformed to years of apartheid policies cannot claim virtue over opponents who brought down those conforming policies.

Neil Postman (1995) cites Americans' remarkable penchant for discourse on education. "There is no intellectual activity more American than quarreling about what education means, especially within the context of school" (p. 139). An important caveat, however, when discussing education, should be an awareness that "while it is possible to speak wisely about education, no one can speak definitively" (Postman, 1995, p. 139).

Speaking definitively about education and other subjects, however, is a skill quite ably honed by Bennett and others. As a remarkable testament to salespersonship (at least in view of the commercial success of Bennett's book) Bennett's own "virtues" seem to be in direct contrast to his "how-to lists" for others. Among Bennett's virtues seem to lie the inability to even communicate with one's "enemies," as illustrated by his widely reported January 1997 hostility toward his party's Speaker of the House Newt Gingrich for Gingrich's invitation to Jesse Jackson to sit in the Speaker's box for the State of the Union speech. The severity of the attack by Bennett upon Gingrich is revealing in many regards. First, Gingrich's national unpopularity makes him an easy target even for those within his own party. To so attack an unpopular man is, apparently, among the virtues we know as "courage." Secondly, Bennett's verbal assault informs us of his belief in the Republican Party as representing "true conservatives" only. A significantly less sizable "big tent" than the Republicans, including Bennett, would have had us believe at their last convention. It appears the Republican Party, if Bennett had his way, would not be an inclusive "big tent," but a rather less inclusive "pup tent." Unless, of course, everyone believed as Bennett does, which, again apparently at least, would make them "virtuous" enough to share his space.

Character education's "fix the kids" orientation is a logical product of the school of thought that believes that kids need fixing (Kohn, 1997). While it seems unlikely that Bennett and others who might teach us "moral virtues" believe that their own children "need fixing," it seems equally likely that those (particularly those who dare to disagree with him and might impart "different" even "liberal" values on to their own children) do.

In marked contrast to the view that kids need fixing, first lady Hillary Rodham Clinton in her book *It Takes a Village* proclaims: "I have never met a stupid child, though I've met plenty of children whom adults insist on calling 'stupid' when the children don't perform in a way that conforms to adult expectations" (1996, p. 239). An approach that aims to "fix the kids" ignores volumes of accumulated evidence from the field of social psychology demonstrating that much of how we act and who we are reflects the situations in which we find ourselves (Kohn, 1997).

If we need to teach our students the "virtues," then perhaps as a prerequisite we might make certain that they understand the concept of "virtue." To actually become virtuous, we must surely realize, is far different from merely learning the virtues.

It is a high calling to seek to "instruct the conscience" of the student. Most of us, for a variety of reasons, settle for trying to "stimulate the intellect" (Meilaender, 1984, p. 75). College professors, certainly, try to "stimulate the intellect." In so doing, it seems, they cannot wholly escape from teaching values. Their values. Just as how we individually spend our disposable income reflects our values, so too does how we individually spend our time.

> Students learn values by observing how professors perform in and outside the classroom—professors who are dispassionate in their search for the truth, careful in their weighing of evidence, respectful in their toleration of disagreement, candid in their confession of error, and considerate and decent in their treatment of other human beings. (Freedman, 1996, p. 57)

Thomas J. Lasley, II (1997) agrees that "values are learned through observation and practice" (p. 655). Social learning complicates any attempt to "teach" values, and in a sound byte that would make a politician proud, Lasley proclaims "values are caught, not taught" (p. 655). Having said that, the impact that faculty members have upon students, while great, should not be overstated:

> Faculty members are reasonably intelligent human beings who have learned to do some things relatively well and who possess traits that can aid in the development of students; they are not necessarily paragons of virtue. (Mayhew, *et al.*, 1990, p. 134)

Chapter One

"The Virtuous Ones"

To begin this venture into "virtuousness" it is necessary to reflect upon the proliferation of "ethical and moral treatises," the recent acceptance through priming of the "virtues" and the "way things ought to be" as determined by some as relayed in these treatises, and the implications this acceptance has upon education and educational "reform" as we prepare to enter the twenty-first century. Foremost among those implications is the further polarization of society generally, and within our educational delivery system in particular. By looking at education within the larger societal context that allows such persons as William Bennett and Rush Limbaugh to advance and gain widespread acceptance for agendas reinstating societal "virtue," we may look critically at the entire concept of teaching "values" and "ethics." Rather than allow the "values" debate to be controlled by those seemingly in favor of greater "individualism" and greater polarization, real "value" reform might only be realized by practicing educational "triage" and stopping the bleeding that prevents so many of our students afflicted with poverty and other harmful impediments to learning from achieving their full potential. We need to understand that "no list of virtues can be made from neutral ground,...any list will reflect beliefs about human nature and its possibilities" (Meilaender, 1984).

It is surely less difficult to teach and/or learn ethics than to practice ethics through living one's life ethically. Education is not so much about what you learn, but about what you become, how you think, and how you live your life. Aristotelian tradition would have us believe that "virtue" is a character trait, a disposition to act in certain ways. It is an important part of the tradition, sometimes lost on persons like Limbaugh particularly, that the exercise of virtue requires judgment that is at least partially the result of education and practice. A good character, however defined, is "not life lived according to a rule (there rarely is a rule by which good qualities ought to be combined or hard choices resolved), it is a life lived in balance" (Wilson, 1993, p. 243).

> This does not mean that students must continually be angst ridden and depressed as they grapple with the moral complexity of the world. But it does mean that they will be encouraged to develop a critical attitude toward almost every aspect of learning—from their interactions on the playground to their discussions with peers in the classroom to their analyses of curricular texts. This critical attitude is seen as essential to developing students' internal "ownership" of what is morally right and wrong. Such an attitude is unlikely to be achieved by Bennett's more externally driven alternative: uncritical absorption of a singular moral perspective. (Fine, 1995, p. 181)

Bennett, it seems, is strongly in favor of emphasizing moral action over thinking; he sees the exercise of moral reflection as incongruent with merely practicing "good moral habits" (Fine, 1995, p. 179). Thinking seems inconsistent with inculcation, which may explain to some degree at least, why Bennett worked to abolish the department of education. Whatever we might learn from the *Book of Virtues*, and to a lesser extent *The Way Things Ought To Be*, we surely might surmise that the authors will do the thinking for us and allow us to spend our time more expeditiously by spreading their unchallenged gospel to the masses. Combining the works of Limbaugh and Bennett seems appropriate enough as each uses the other as an endorser upon their books' respective jackets. Bennett's view of himself and others with whom he agrees is also quite ably summed up in an article in which he refers to Limbaugh as "possibly our greatest living American" (Eastland, 1992, p. 23). The fact that these two men share each others views is, I'm sure, merely coincidental to being among our "greatest living Americans."

Do What I Say and We'll All Get Along Just Fine

The issue of control and, most importantly, who controls the debate over "virtue," lies at the heart of instilling "virtues." Like a bank robber in the old western movies of days gone by, those who tell us "do as I say and nobody will get hurt" remind us of a simpler time.

Nothing could be so simple as an emphasis upon "top-down" mandates with Bennett and those who think like him at the "top." Alfie Kohn (1997) describes these top-down mandates as what passes for character education nowadays: "A collection of exhortations and extrinsic inducements designed to make children work harder and do what they're told...the point is to drill students in specific behaviors rather than engage them in deep, critical reflection about certain ways and being" (p. 429).

Larry Cuban adds, "Specialists write scripts for teachers to use in the classrooms" (1992, p. 31). "Policymakers in the 1980s framed the complex problems of public schooling as an inefficient and ineffective system in need of tightening up, that is, in need of higher standards, more resources, better staffing, and accountability" (Cuban, 1992, p. 45).

Given our capitalistic society, individuals are presupposed to be those whose well-being may well be achieved in ways which detract from the overall social well-being. To demand virtue of such an individual is to ask for a quite inexplicable altruism: a sacrifice of much of what her life is devoted to (Poole, 1991). To expect altruism from society, while practicing and lauding unabashed capitalism in all its forms, seems at least somewhat idealistic, if not actually hypocritical. Understanding the context requires that we collectively and carefully examine the largely self-righteous "virtues" of those who hope to impose their "virtuousness" upon the rest of us. Within that examination we may discover that adherence to their plans for reinstating virtue and reforming various public endeavours might actually promote further polarization and cause significant long-term harm to those already on the outside looking in.

> Community, added to individualism, brought us unprecedented strength, the strength of a diverse group of people setting aside their lack of shared blood, faith, traditions, and heirarchies to work together for the common good. When the danger is clear and present, we pull together superbly. But in the intervals between crises, our strong streak of individualism often overpowers us and encourages us to behave as though we were capable of surviving and thriving as 250 million disassociated entities. (Cuomo, 1995, p. 72)

The temptation to look to "virtue" reminds those cognizant of history of the examples of rigidly heirarchical civilizations which have invoked their citizenry to support their virtues less as a means of bettering society than as a means of restricting those below from questioning those in control. It is no secret that Bennett and others like him have partisan interests that have reflected beliefs that are wholly inconsistent with the beliefs of many others in our society. Beliefs which, if allowed to flourish, might further strengthen the hands dealt to the most favored in our society, while weakening those below.

The answer to our problems does not lie in an infusion of "values" into the national psyche. "Along that path lies the elimination of enemies and the enforcement of orthodoxy, the end of history and the final solution" (Scott, 1996, p. 178).

Priming and Uncritical Absorption

The "clear and present" danger presented by the phenomenon of priming lies in the unwavering and accepting receipt of the "information" presented. If we continue to condemn our MTV generation, and the apparent attention-span deficiencies that, while not created by MTV, are symbolically linked with it, then in fairness we ought to attempt to understand possible harmful results of other mediums that target other audiences and that tend to capitalize upon our society's limited desire to delve deeply into issues. Ultimately the effect of such discourse upon social policy, including but not limited to education, will be very difficult to overcome in the standard political arena, where "priming" has been and continues to be most effective.

The understanding of "priming" begins by accepting evidence from research indicating that when people make judgments or decisions, they rarely take into consideration the entire array of available relevant evidence. Common sense also tells us that we all, to differing degrees, tend to use whatever mental shortcuts are available, rather than assess and analyze each possible alternative when considering an approach to remedy a problem. Because of the cognitive burdens imposed by a comprehensive information search followed by a careful integration process, people tend to "satisfice" rather than "optimize" (see Simon, 1957; Simon & Stedry, 1968). Put another way, people often derive their decisions from limited bits of the larger pool of available information so as to make satisfactory judgments without putting forth tremendous effort (Krosnick & Brannon, 1993). Anthony R. Pratkanis and Eliot Aronson (1992) call this the "essential dilemma of modern democracy" (p. 31).

On the one hand, we, as a society, value persuasion; our government is based on the belief that free speech and discussion and exchange of ideas can lead to fairer and better decision making. On the other hand, as cognitive misers we often do not participate fully in this discussion, relying instead not on careful thought and scrutiny of a message, but on simplistic persuasion devices and limited reasoning. Mindless propaganda, not thoughtful persuasion, flourishes. (p. 31)

When so little intellectual effort is put forth, it is impossible to overstate the long-term harm that may be done to sound social and educational policy, "virtuous" or otherwise. Thomas Sowell (1995) lamented the emphasis and effect we as a society allow what he called a "prevailing vision." To Sowell, a prevailing vision means a vision in which the assumptions upon which the vision is based are so much taken for granted by so many people, including so-called "thinking people," that neither those assumptions nor their corollaries are generally confronted with demands for empirical evidence (1995, p. 2).

Robert Bork, ill-fated Supreme Court nominee, provides several examples of his "prevailing vision" in his book *Slouching Towards Gomorrah*, which is provocatively subtitled: "Modern Liberalism and American Decline." Among the statements within the book is the following concerning crime prevention programs: "...midnight basketball is so obviously a frivolous notion that it need not be discussed..." (p. 166). Such anti-intellectualism should not reign whether or not a given program has merit. In the case of midnight basketball, many leading criminologists, as well as leading mainstream publications, such as *Time* (August 22, 1994) and *Sports Illustrated* (August 19, 1996) have gone on record as praising midnight basketball and citing instances of its success in urban areas. Bork, one of the annointed surely, proclaims, no doubt for our benefit and all readers of his work— who are, I presume "true believers" of his—that what he does not believe in is "so obviously frivolous a notion that it need not be discussed." Although even his detractors generally cite his intelligence, Bork seems to present himself as a vivid example of a primer, guilty not of conservatism, but of conceptual conservatism. He "knows" that he is right and therefore discussion of issues with which he disagrees is unnecessary. Bork buttresses his opinions by citing equally annointed "primers" such as Bennett and Charles Murray in his work.

The results of short-sighted decision-making tend to be borne out over time and, depending upon the weight of given decisions, are thrust upon the heads of the next generation. Lewis H. Lapham (1993) proclaims that "most of the country's present trouble follows from the blind arrogance of too many people in power and the apathy and lack of objection on the part of too many people out of power" (p. 37). It is the apparent apathy of so many of us who do not "object" to wrongs committed by our own government which ultimately bear upon our children in the form of poverty, educational underfunding, crime, and urban decay. Uninformed opinions which too often are passed on as "facts" contribute to wrongheaded governmental policy through the pressures placed upon our elected officials, and their all too frequent desire to appeal to the majority of voters, despite what may be their own better judgment. Pratkanis and Aronson (1992) refer to "factoids" as:

> ...assertions of fact that are not backed up by evidence, usually because the fact is false or because evidence in support of the assertion cannot be obtained. Factoids are presented in such a manner that they become widely treated as true. (p. 71)

Many of the most firmly held and therefore most potentially harmful "factoids" concern education and educational policy.

> Education is one of those issues about which many people have strong opinions. This is because almost everyone has been subjected to education. Interestingly, those who tend to express the strongest views tend to be those on whom the

experience has had the least lasting effect. The truly educated person should understand how ambiguous are the goals of education, and how complex the means to be used to reach those goals. (Reich, 1989, p. 96)

The importance of our national educational policy and philosophy will play a pivotal role in future funding, future court decisions impacting education, and ultimately the education our children receive. Stanley Elam (1995) laments our seeming inability to recognize the need for equal access to education. If we don't give everyone equal access to knowledge,

> ...we are likely to have an ever-widening disparity between the haves and have-nots, more elitism and conspicuous consumption, more racial conflicts as minorities become the majority before the year 2100, more social chaos, and another million incarcerated young people—the continuing scandal of modern-day America. (Elam, 1995, p. 28)

Mortimer Adler also comments,

> Since children have significant differences in their economic, social, and ethnic backgrounds and especially differences in the homes from which they come, they probably need differing schoolhouse experiences. Differences in children's innate endowment can likely be overcome through the use of new educational devices and methods. Differences, however, in children's home and family circumstances will require that greater efforts be made. The choice then is to abandon the effort to carry out the educational mandate of a truly democratic society, or to require society to undertake economic and social as well as educational reforms to facilitate carrying out that mandate. (Adler, 1977, p. 134)

David C. Berliner and Bruce J. Biddle's *The Manufactured Crisis* (1995) goes a long way toward dispelling many of the myths of our "failing educational system" perpetuated so ably by those opposing much of what public schooling stands for—greater equality and greater equality of opportunity. Presidents

Ronald Reagan and George Bush, assisted by their secretaries of education, endlessly cited the unprecedented "problems" of the public schools. As in *A Nation at Risk*, most of these claims were said to reflect evidence, "although the evidence in question either was not presented or appeared in the form of simplistic, misleading generalizations" (Berliner & Biddle, 1995, p. 3). Joel Spring (1988) took the view that "most education reports in the 80's were using public schools as scapegoats for economic problems caused by factors outside the realm of education" (pp. 58-9). Berliner and Biddle as well as Spring viewed the "failings" of our economy as resting more upon the shoulders of business than with the public schools. Donovan Walling (1995) likewise referred to *A Nation at Risk* as a "misguided political initiative largely aimed at making public education the scapegoat for society's ills" (p. 34). Making public education a "scapegoat" for the ills of society may very well have been a method used by those anti-public school factions that sought a lessening of public support for education. Such a diminishment in public support might assist those, like Bennett, who sought and continue to seek greater government support of "their" programs assisting private schools.

It shouldn't take tremendous detective skills to recognize that a group of people largely intent on vouchers and other initiatives to strengthen private and/or christian education at the expense of public education might overstate the "failings" of public education. The mystery lies not in these attempts, but rather in the media's and subsequently the public's acceptance of these myths as gospel. "Surely a major reason for increased criticism of schools in the 1980s was that reactionary voices were given more credence in America during that decade. When Americans elected Ronald Reagan, and afterwards George Bush to the presidency, they made the expression of right-wing ideologies fashionable" (Berliner & Biddle, 1995, p. 132). Berliner and Biddle refer to "ideologues on the right" who had "long been critical of the public schools" as gaining legitimacy upon the conservative taking of the presidency. These "ideologues" included persons such as "moralists" like Bennett and later Limbaugh, whose influence continued to grow as illustrated by their own increasing production of books, television shows, and appearances, prominent "news" magazine articles, and so forth. The increasing "legitimacy" of these persons was given prominence by the press, which naturally led to a widespread public "acceptance" of the conclusions within *A Nation at Risk*, and other "conservative" creations of the era.

A Nation at Risk "merely gave public voice to charges about education that right-wing ideologues had already been telling one another. Thus it served to publicize tenets of conservative educational thought and was, as a result, embraced with enthusiasm by right-wing troops in the Reagan White House" (Berliner & Biddle, 1995, p. 140). As further evidence of the influence of the "true believers" the "incidentals" within the report, such as the belief that teachers salaries needed to be raised and that the federal government actually needed to take a greater role in funding public education, were conveniently ignored in favor of public proclamations lamenting the "failures" of public education and arguing in favor of voucher systems and other aids to private education. It is truly an interesting phenomenon, to me at least, that we have the innate ability to recognize a problem (too little funding, too low pay) and then seek its solution in ways that have nothing to do with increasing funding and increasing pay. It's as if we see a broken window in our home and decide that the way to "conserve heat" is to spend money on insulating the attic. Fixing the broken window would be for people who apparently don't entirely recognize the "greater failures" within the system. The more one reads about the educational "crisis" the more one becomes quite understandably confused about where the "heat" is being lost.

Priming as a Dangerous Phenomenon

Aside from the obvious shortcomings of decision-making based on a limited review of the facts, the real danger in priming lies in the lasting impact of the flawed decisions ultimately made. "We often respond to propaganda with little thought and in a mindless fashion" (Pratkanis & Aronson, 1991, p. 26). While not standing alone as a "primer," perhaps no better example exists in public view today than the "Rush Limbaugh Phenomenon." Whether or not mass media phenomena such as Limbaugh will last significantly beyond the life expectancy of most fads (and his recent abandonment of his television show seems to indicate that his star is fading), the widespread knowledge of and belief in the phenomena make it a worthwhile subject for our consideration as it belies a growing weakness in our society, namely the growth and acceptance of priming. When the thrust of political priming largely concerns a president with "character flaws" acknowledged even by his own supporters, the result is, and has been, misinformation accepted as true information on a rather grand scale.

"Issues that have been the subject of extensive attention on television and radio and in newspapers are particularly likely to come to citizens' minds shortly thereafter and thereby to enjoy enhanced impact on...evaluations" (Krosnick & Brannon, 1993, p. 168). The distinction between "news" and "entertainment" has become so cloudy that all too often the "postmodern imagination is a product of the mass media" (Lapham, 1993, p. 160).

In accordance with the heart of priming, it is the widespread "acceptance" of the gospel according to persons like Limbaugh that should be of concern, far more than any specific preaching from that gospel. Whatever side of the political spectrum one is on, the danger to social policy of Limbaugh and those like him lies in their ability to persuasively communicate "facts" which may or may not be true, but are, in either event, uncritically accepted by a significant number of persons. Eric Hoffer wrote about "true believers" long before Limbaugh came upon the scene, but it is Limbaugh who perhaps best illustrates the impact that an influential public figure can have without any real standing and often tenuous at best factual support underlying his opinions.

Chapter Two

"I Am What I Am—Aren't I?"

"Virtues" and "Intelligence" Are Largely in the Eye of the Beholder

It is in this context that I suggest that William Bennett is to virtues as ketchup is to a vegetable. While Bennett is no doubt endowed with many virtuous traits, just as ketchup is endowed with many of the traits of a vegetable, to suppose that both are the same is to take a great deal of liberty with otherwise recognized common sense. While we should all be free to read the works of whomever we like, we should place a person's writings in the context of his or her life and agenda. In Bennett's case, his role as Secretary of Education was used as a bully pulpit from which he preached, among other things, the "virtue" of abandoning the public schools in favor of private schools. As Secretary of Education under President Ronald Reagan, Bennett spoke on Pat Robertson's "700 Club" television show and urged parents to protest their schools' curriculum. He was so suspect of public education that he spoke to the Carolina Policy Council, a right-wing organization hostile to the very concept of public education (Fine, 1995).

Bennett has also called on the schools to "foster a national consensus in support of the Reagan Administration policy in Central America" (Starr, 1989, p. 98). Whether or not "virtues" are non-partisan, Bennett is surely among our most partisan political influences, and failure to recognize his partisanship is a failure to fully consider the merits of his call to virtue. Among his first public statements as Secretary of Education was to call for sharp cuts in the federal student-loan program. He followed that by calling for "deregulation" of the principal's job so that it might be opened up to noneducators (Starr, 1989, p. 98). One suspects that these noneducators would be those successful in business and other apparently more "worthwhile" pursuits. With a friend like that as Secretary of Education, teachers quite rightfully became even more defensive about their roles in the educational system of the future. Given this prior knowledge of Bennett's record, it is with great trepidation that we should consider his "call to virtue" as anything beyond a continuation of the division of America into one country for the advantaged and one for the disadvantaged, however thinly veiled as the less "virtuous."

> The first step in moving toward greater social justice through education is to avoid the premature polarizations that arise when educational policy is confused with political ideology. In the United States today, the hostile political split between liberals and conservatives has infected the public debate over education—to such an extent that straight thinking is made difficult. (Hirsch, 1996, p. 5)

It might seem as if, to some extent at least, Bennett's credibility and to a greater extent, Rush Limbaugh's credibility, have been "manufactured."

> Instead of thinking about important issues for ourselves, we turn to credible-looking leaders for their solutions. This strat-

egy would make some sense if the people we turn to indeed possess the required expertise. Sadly, it is often the case that credibility has been subtly manufactured and sold for propaganda purposes. (Pratkanis & Aronson, 1991, p. 105)

Bennett is harshly lampooned by Jon Katz (1997) for his 1980s roles as drug czar and education secretary.

Drug policy and deteriorating schools are acknowledged to be two of the more tragic public policy disasters in modern memory. ...in other cultures...Bennett might have left the public arena in shame or thrown himself upon an ancestral blade...but in shame-free America, extreme failure in pursuit of self-righteousness is no vice.... Bennett now serves as our reigning, if self-appointed, national virtues czar. (p. 22)

Katz continues, holding no punches:

Bennett may be at a loss to know how to stop drugs, improve schools or end the slaughter of kids on city streets, but he has an unerring sense of the yearning many adults have for simple definitions of right and wrong to preach to their kids. (p. 23)

For all the Republican insistence on liberal responsibility for the decline in virtue, the first publication of *Playboy* (1953), the first pelvic gyrations of Elvis Presley, and the controversial federal judicial ruling in favor of the publication of *Lady Chatterley's Lover* (1959) came during the Eisenhower era. More recently and more significantly, George Bush in 1992 followed up a Republican convention that saluted family values with an autumn campaign in which he happily appeared before crowds with two Hollywood stars most prominently in tow—Bruce Willis of *Die Hard 2*, a movie with a total body count of 264, and Arnold Schwarzenegger, who gunned down 17 policemen in *The Terminator* and bellowed "Consider this a divorce!" just before he shot his wife in *Total Recall*. Social commentator Christopher Lasch has touched on a further hypocrisy:

Republicans may hate what is happening to our children, but

their commitment to the culture of acquisitive individualism makes them reluctant to probe its source. They glorify the man on the make, the small operator who stops at nothing in the pursuit of wealth, and then wonder why ghetto children steal and hustle instead of applying themselves to homework. (Phillips, 1994, p. 63)

It was among Dan Quayle's proudest "achievements" to be directing the President's "council on competitiveness" which attempted to eliminate what the administration considered "hampering restrictions" upon business, such as several provisions of the Clean Air Act. The "virtue" of such an achievement would surely be viewed differently depending upon whether you are a hampered business person or a person more concerned with inhaling the air around a business now somewhat less hampered by such restrictions. So which is it? Is it more virtuous to allow business greater freedom or is it more virtuous to allow citizens greater freedom from businesses' intrusions into the environment? The answer it seems, appears to have everything to do with whose "virtues" are deemed most important.

One's virtues have, of course, everything to do with one's values that have been shaped by life experiences common only to each individual. One's values have long been considered as one of the bases for decisions. The problem for us societally comes when one's virtues as shaped by those values become accepted and unquestioned because of the status, real or perceived, of the messenger and/or the medium. Often, the medium has self-interests that override those of the group. Organizational theory, in fact, has a strong tradition of emphasizing the importance of individuals' self-interests and the occasional conflict with organizational interests (see *e.g.* Weiss, 1995). Bennett and others seem to fit this pattern of emphasizing similarly situated self-interest over the interests of the larger society. Educators have long struggled with the question of whether education should be structured so as to develop the potentialities of each individual, or whether it should be structured to attain and preserve the interests of the larger society (Rorty, 1993).

Charles Murray and Richard Herrnstein argue, as do many on either side of the political spectrum, that America faces widening inequalities and a solidifying class structure. Such recognition of a growing disparity is hardly arguable any longer, but Murray and Herrnstein go further, to also argue that intelligence, rather than background or social status, is the most powerful determinant of poverty and as such it is intelligence (or a lack thereof) that is widely responsible for a swathe of our most serious social problems, ranging from crime to unemployment and welfare dependency.

Adults not only predict children's fates based on risk factors such as poverty and single parenthood, but they often assign children—even very young children—certain fates based on what they perceive as the children's fixed characteristics and abilities. Sometimes children who are combative and provocative, for example, are labeled hyperactive or simply as problem children, labels that are passed on year after year and that worm themselves into children's self-perceptions. Sometimes children are tagged as slow learners or as socially unskilled, tags that can have similarly large and lasting consequences. In these cases prophecies often become self-fulfilling. It is notoriously difficult, for example, for children placed in remedial tracks or special education classes to move upward or into the mainstream. Books such as Herrnstein and Murray's *The Bell Curve* suggest that we should limit the resources invested in the intellectual development of young children who appear, based on IQ scores, to have limited potential (Weissbourd, 1996, pp. 38-9). Hillary Rodham Clinton (1996) suggests that the conclusions within *The Bell Curve* are not only unscientific (as suggested by many, notably Berliner & Biddle, 1995, p. 46) but also insidious. "It is increasingly apparent that the nature-nurture question is not an 'either/or' debate so much as a 'both/and' proposition" (Clinton, 1996, p. 59).

> Those who argue that our nation cannot afford to implement
> comprehensive early education programs for disadvantaged
> children and their families...are not acting on the evidence but
> according to a different agenda. (Clinton, 1996, p. 61)

The evidence, according to David C. Berliner and Bruce J.
Biddle (1995), among others, is that "there are literally hundreds
of studies demonstrating the sizable effects of social environment on measured IQ" (p. 46). Despite the fact that these studies
are widely known and understood in the large community of
social researchers in intelligence, Herrnstein and Murray either
seem to have misinterpreted volumes of data, or have simply
ignored it altogether in an effort to justify biases and bigotry that
has been in existence for decades. Perhaps the thought of sharing
the advantages of education with the "common people" is simply
too much to bear. After all, if everyone were entitled to a college
education, or if everyone had genuine equal access, how would
some persons continue to maintain their proper "place" at the top
of our society?

There are many reasons to recoil in horror when presented
with "beliefs" concerning the rather subjectively measured IQs
and/or virtues of our citizens. Among those fears may lie the
horrible recognition that those of us who have not fully realized
our "potential" may in fact just be less intelligent. Such a fear,
however, is tempered by simple common sense and scores of
anecdotal examples that seem to contradict any high-IQ-equals-
success corrollation. Any person living in America in the last
decade and a half during which Dan Quayle rose to the vice-
presidency, Ronald Reagan to the presidency, and Clarence
Thomas to the Supreme Court should readily come to the
conclusion that whatever factor their IQs may or may not have
been in their ascendency, it may have had more to do with
background, political connections, ambition, and simple luck.
Income is, or can be, similarly obtained: "much income and
wealth comes with slight or no social justification, little or no

economic service on the part of the recipient" (Galbraith, 1996, p. 61). Laurence Shames (1991, p. 185) spoke of "letting the marketplace decide" and the injustices that occur when that marketplace decides that lawyers are worth several times more than teachers, and baseball players dozens of times more than teachers, and CEOs often several dozens of times more than the average worker. The "wisdom" of the marketplace doesn't always appear to be compatible with common sense, nor with "virtue." Allowing the marketplace to "decide" issues of "worth," however, does allow us to abdicate any responsibility we might have in looking at equity issues. Talk about the "Dumbing down of America," letting the marketplace make all decisions allows for a "virtuous" society of million dollar ballplayers and lowly paid schoolteachers.

Do High IQs Equal Success?

High level politicians are but one highly visible example of persons rising well beyond where their apparent IQs might have "justifiably" taken them. Another even more significant reason to discount the "high-IQ-equals-success" theory lies in our inability to assess IQ as an unambiguous and readily interpretable innate trait. To suppose, based on words and actions alone, that the IQs of Reagan, Quayle, and Thomas are either less than or more than the average citizen is to be guilty of rampant and unproductive speculation. Likewise then, it is not productive to anecdotally cite examples of "intelligent" persons who have not risen, and "intellectually lesser" individuals who have; instead it is the very thought that such a "justifiable distribution" occurs that should bother all of us regardless of our individual IQ.

The ultimate harm of focusing on ambiguous criteria as a determination of "the failure of our present system" lies in how such criteria shape our views of those with whom we share little in common. Viewing the disadvantaged as less "virtuous" or less "intelligent" is painfully arrogant, misinformed, and ultimately dangerously divisive. Such a view totally neglects the environmental factors that often lead to poverty, substance abuse, crime, and educational inequality while concentrating instead on ambiguous and ill-defined "traits" that may or may not be associated with those persons afflicted with such ills.

"Virtue through Achievement Is Often Less Than It Appears"

Former Texas Governor Ann Richards once said of former President Bush: "He was born at third base, and he thinks he hit a home run." While her political rhetoric might be overly harsh, a larger point Richards made lies in the degree of acceptance of achievement as one's just desserts, and the necessary simultaneous and opposite belief that others' lack of achievement is equally others' just desserts. Likewise, there has been an increasing tendency to accept the words of "achievers" in this country who have no experience with or quite possibly even understanding of those for whom they seek to set social policy. Many of those preaching "family values," greater "virtue," and other valuable societal traits, have had little contact with persons outside of their socioeconomic strata, which not so surprisingly is at the highest levels of income. If one was born at third base, it seems all too easy to forget why others reside at first base and how difficult it might be for them to reach a third base level of "success."

The hypocracy that most of us (myself included) are capable of in viewing the actions of others versus our own is among the problems that face us societally as we attempt to impose or restore our "virtues" upon others with whom we have little in common. An example of such hypocritical thought lies in the "qualifications" we require of some, but not of others. Many in this country view President Bill Clinton's lack of wartime service as a disqualifying factor in his ability to lead our armed forces, while many of the same people give nary a thought to the ability of Bennett, Limbaugh, Bush, Reagan, Quayle, Newt Gingrich, and others so fortunate, to direct and "reform" our educational and welfare policy that most directly impacts those with whom they have the least in common. A remarkably simple example of what appears to be rampant hypocracy lies in the popular rhetoric of many within our country expressing concern over the abilities of Clinton, a former governor who has not served in the military, to effectively and credibly lead our troops. Interestingly, whatever the validity or invalidity of such a concern, many of the people openly expressing it had every confidence in the national defense ability of a similarly inexperienced Reagan.

Even more troubling still than *whom* we seem to allow great influence, is our high-rate of acceptance of the philosophy that there might be a singular path toward "virtue." The reality is that there is not one single ethic or one single path, and consequently our desire to search for such a non-existent path is time and effort consuming, but extremely unproductive, if not actually counter-productive.

> In society as in farming, monoculture works poorly. It exhausts the soil. The social richness of America comes from the diversity of its tribes. Its capacity for cohesion, for some spirit of common agreement on what is to be done, comes from the willingness of those tribes not to elevate their cultural differences into impassable barriers and ramparts. (Hughes, 1993, p. 14)

"Reading America is like scanning a mosaic. If you only look at the big picture, you do not see its parts—the distinct glass tiles, each a different color. If you concentrate only on tiles, you cannot see the picture" (Hughes, 1993, p. 14). If we want to truly enjoy the beauty of this mosaic, rather than trying to get all the tiles to conform, we need to allow all of the tiles a chance to adhere to a sound and sturdy base. It is that influential persons among us, rather than those more qualified, might ultimately decide what that sturdy base should be that is so daunting and, at times, so frightening a prospect. Again Katz (1997) effectively summarizes the danger in his portrayal of Bennett:

> It wouldn't matter so much if Bennett were just the latest in a long line of hustlers hawking potions to prolong life, shrink tumors, and cure impotence. But his predecessors didn't advise office-holders and -seekers or dream of taking themselves or their wares so seriously. Bennett takes himself very seriously, and is taken seriously by others. (p. 27)

"Do unto Others"

The truly intractable difficulty of American education today lies not in its ideological content, or with the IQs or "virtues" of our youth, but rather with the state of preparedness of its students. "This problem lies far back, in the high schools, where 'disadvantaged' students—mainly black—receive a basic education that is shockingly inferior to white ones" (Hughes, 1993, p. 61). The same difficulty might lie in our society as a whole and its growing infestation with crime, poverty, and devisiveness. It is not the IQs of our youth that should concern us, but rather the policies that we put forward to deal with the problems faced by citizens, young and old.

Similarly, it is not the virtues of the students that put the nation at risk so much as it is the virtues of a nation that continues to all but ignore the problems faced by those in the bottom one-third of our society. Practicing what we preach might be a good place to begin our climb toward a more "virtuous" society. To expect more tolerance, more compassion, and more societal contribution from the bottom one-third may be unfair so long as we in the top two-thirds continue to practice less tolerance, less compassion, and less of a "taxing" contribution toward "them." In recent years, we've masterfully used terms like "enabling," "dependence," and phrases such as the "cycle of poverty," to justify our unwillingness to confront our most serious social problems. Our desire to "end welfare as we know it" comes largely from the fact that most of us don't actually "know welfare."

> Those of us who have everything we need and, in general, make all the decisions about our society simply do not know those who are living in poverty, alienation, and despair. The families who find it difficult to get good jobs, decent homes, safe neighborhoods, and good medical care and education do not know or trust their privileged neighbors, the court system, or the police to care about their plight. (Carter, 1996, p. 123)

It isn't merely welfare recipients who feel the wrath of our "virtuous" if not entirely "corporatized" society. Workers, as well, are increasingly living in an age in which "labor has come to be viewed not as a long-term resource but as an expendable cost center" (Kuttner, 1997, p. 74).

> Large corporations are pursuing strategies of retaining as few core employees as possible, pursuing the maximum possible degree of flexibility in how they take on labor. Consultants offer seminars on how to convert a large portion of the work force from permanent staff to contingent employees. (Kuttner, 1997, p. 75)

Contingent employees, of course, are owed little, if any, beyond a day's wage for a day's work. Whether or not this is "virtuous" depends, I suppose, upon your alignment with workers or management. Still, it seems in a culture so dependent upon the economic bottom line that "virtue" has been largely displaced by the very same people so lamenting its decline. Robert Kuttner entitled his book *Everything For Sale*. This section might have expanded upon that phrase to include "everything must go— including the workers."

Chapter Three

"The Virtue of Schools"

It is within this larger and divisive environment, from which educators have been dodging bullets of criticism from all sides, and in which virtue is often synonomous with privilege, that defenders of the public schools generally, and of teaching more specifically, find themselves. Schools continue to be a war zone, often literally, and almost always figuratively.

> When on the one hand, the president of Citizens for Excellence in Education (the activist wing of the National Association of Christian Educators) mused strategically about getting "an active Christian parents committee in operation in all American school districts, so we can take control of all local school boards," and when, on the other hand, the legal director of the ACLU asked for financial support for its "longstanding effort to protect nonsectarian education from the meddling of the fundamentalist right," there is all but a formal declaration of war over the public schools. (Hunter, 1991, p. 197)

James Davison Hunter (1991) further states that "it is because of the intrinsic link between public education, community and national identity, and the future (symbolized by children) that the institutions of education have long been a political and legal battleground" (p. 198). Ivor F. Goodson (1995) similarly refers to the battles waged by varying social groups and forces over the "contested terrain" that is and has been the school.

It is this battleground or "contested terrain" inhabited by many children of differing needs with which we societally must come to grips. The best way to "heal the sick and dying" is to practice triage in the same manner that any field hospital must. We need to locate those in need of the most attention and continue to tend to the wounds of all on the battlefield in descending order of their needs, with those doing the most bleeding receiving the most aid.

If a significant number of Americans abandon public education—either out of lethargy or by opting for private religious, ethnic, or elite academies—we risk turning public schools into schools of last resort (Meier, 1995, p. 5).

> Schools can squelch intelligence, they can foster intolerance and disrespect, and they affect the way we see ourselves in the pecking order. But that's precisely why we cannot abandon our public responsibility to all children, why we need a greater not a lesser commitment to public education. (Meier, 1995, p. 6)

Fairness Is a Prerequisite to Progress

Not so long ago, educational disputes were concerned with equality and race. Recently, the broad ideological shift to the right has concentrated the public's attention instead upon educational standards. While it is difficult to credibly argue against "standards" if any sense of fairness is to exist, then any "standards" that might be implemented should stand upon a firm base of fairness in treatment. If success is to be judged by easily recognized test scores, or other concrete measures, then we must first concentrate on leveling the playing field for all students so that the chosen standards will have value.

In our society, so obsessed with winning, we have allowed for the perversion of even the simple concept of fairness. In our obsession with winning and with standards, we have decided that persons on the losing end of our educational system should somehow be punished for losing. However sad that might be, it becomes worse when we consider that in today's schools many of the players start the game already behind. When these players fail to overcome the tremendous odds and ultimately lose the game, we often decide that we have somehow coddled them and created their dependency. We then are able to convince ourselves that the only fair thing to do is to lessen any aid they may have received and require them to pull their own weight. What many of us fail to recognize is that the burdens faced by the poor have become an insurmountable weight that they carry each day, and that expecting them to overcome the odds without our assistance is as blatantly unfair as allowing one team to start an athletic contest behind by twenty points. Even if somehow the poor overcome the odds and only end up losing the game by fifteen points we still adhere to "standards" that tell us only a "final score" by which we can readily identify winners and losers.

The decade of the 1980s, in which the quest for standards heightened, gave us a not-so-hidden assumption among many that the quest for equality had produced a threatening erosion of public school standards (Katznelson & Weir, 1985). Whatever factor or factors that one considers the leading cause of our "decline," there is ample reason to believe that the schools, even if they share a large burden of responsibility, do not deserve all of the blame. To blame the schools disproportionately seems to be "scapegoating" in its most pure form.

Education is not the problem, it is as it always has been, the solution, and our society's second most successful "gateway to opportunity" (Goodwin, 1992, p. 146). While the most successful "gateway to opportunity" continues to be inheritance and the accident of birth, education is still our greatest hope for creating opportunity, just as a lack of education can take opportunity away (Goodwin, 1992). "The decisions we make concerning public education in this country could mean the difference between reestablishing the United States as the land of opportunity and becoming even more decisively a land of haves and have-nots" (Greider, 1992, p. 73). "Supporting the public schools is about living the values which the school stands for, whatever one's age" (Sizer, 1992, p. 27). This is the rhetoric that many might hope would be on the lips of teachers, administrators, and parents, not the social Darwinism made so popular by Ronald Reagan and now practiced without apology by Newt Gingrich and the Republican-controlled Congress.

Social Darwinism has recently touched many aspects of American life. Perhaps it always has. Still, if what is good for General Motors is indeed good for America, it seems as though the 1980s in particular saw a rather significant departure in the way General Motors, as an example, conducted its business. It was this era that ushered in a new habit that began to spread through corporate America, a tradition of declining loyalty of firm to worker and a consequent wariness among younger employees of depending upon any job for permanent security (Newman, 1993). American culture is based in large part on an underlying social Darwinism that sees justice in the rule of survival of the fittest. We believe that those who are well equipped to compete will reap material rewards and that, conversely, those who cannot "cut the mustard" will (and should) suffer deprivation (Newman, 1993, p. 18).

Since we cannot change, at least without tremendous intrusion, the educational environment within the homes in which our children live, we should strive to make certain that once those children enter the schoolhouse, they may have a decent, safe, and valuable experience. An experience that might instill in them and ultimately in their children the value that we as a nation place upon education.

While We Value High IQs, We Devalue Education

While we focus upon restoring "virtue," seemingly in spite of education, the extent to which education is genuinely valued in our society has often been called into question (Gardner, 1991). Consistent with our society's love of money and our dependence upon inheritance and privilege, we value what some have been given far more than we value that which some have earned. While there is probably not a sinister plot to keep the poor oppressed, the result of less government involvement will certainly prolong the oppression just as surely as if it were a conscious plot on behalf of the wealthy.

"The educational enterprise continues to be devalued by our society, our academic institutions, and even by us...part of the problem is caused by the simplistic way we think about it" (Weimer, 1993, p. 2).

> How can something so central to the mission of our institution, so intrinsically a part of the advancement of knowledge, be given such short shrift? The answer is complicated, but I am firmly convinced that the lack of reward and recognition in part results from the simplistic,nonreflective, and uninformed ways many in our profession think about teaching. Approaching the teaching-learning enterprise in more intellectually robust ways puts you on the side of those of us committed to being part of the solution. (Weimer, 1993, p. 124)

For the federal government to abdicate responsibility and argue that states know best is to abandon any precept that we want all of our children to stand a fair, if perhaps not equal, chance in this country regardless of where they were born. Amy Gutmann (1987) argues that "a democratic state must take steps to avoid...inequalities that deprive children of educational attainment adequate to participate in the political process" (p. 134).

We have been deluding ourselves, as a nation, by failing to recognize the impact upon all of us that "poor" education has. Although a poorly educated student may not live in "my" neighborhood, or have daily contact with me, my taxes and ultimately my lifestyle will be impacted adversely by that student's eventual lack of ability and productivity, as well as the ultimate failure to attain for himself or herself the level that a good education might have made possible. Connections have been made between "poor" education and increased crime (see _inter alia_ Hirschi, 1972; West & Farrington, 1973). Other studies claim that "poor" educational opportunities or the failure of the educational system to meet the needs of constituents leads to increased dependency and decreased productivity; but despite our knowledge of the connection, we seem all too able to ignore any connections that do not presently and directly impact us.

As early as 1790, Noah Webster wrote that "it is much easier to introduce and establish an effectual system for preserving morals than to correct by penal statutes the ill effects of a bad system." All too often in the political debate of the moment, we concentrate our intellectual efforts on capital punishment, "three strikes and you're out," and other penal methods, and neglect any "preventative maintenance" that might lessen problems that arise or even eliminate many problems before they arise. Recent House Republican efforts have been effective at ridiculing such prevention efforts as "midnight basketball" and "Americorps." Conservatives have been able to argue that these prevention programs have not been adequately "proven" to reduce crime. This same "proof requirement" of effectiveness is apparently not needed when capital punishment or greater prison space is considered.

At the center of the lives of our children lie two institutions that have a dominant influence upon their lives, their families and their schools. Little can effectively be done to ensure loving and educational environments at home, but much can be done to improve the "care" of our children in our schools. "Public schools are one of the major institutions that bind Americans together and that support democracy" (McElvaine, 1987, p. 127). Almost a century ago, John Dewey wrote of the importance of a communal perspective on education and referred to the school as a "small society" (Driscoll, 1995). Policies which seek to lessen the importance of public schooling and which allow the federal government to approach a "hands-off" attitude toward public education go hand in hand with tax and social policies that seek divisions among the people.

To accept the premise that "free market competition" will make a better "product" is to cast off millions of American children in schools that are unable or unwilling to compete. If there is some merit to competition, then poorly managed schools should be given incentives to be better managed, and likewise, disincentives should exist for poor schools. Unfortunately, unlike business, it will not be "poor" products that will be cast off so that better products may survive; it instead will be "poor" children who are cast aside, and that is a loss to all of us, both directly and indirectly.

"Doing the Right Thing: Whether It's Spending or Investment"

In the face of scarce resources, persons in government now commonly refer to spending as "investment," as a way of cushioning the blow delivered to those who view any money sent outward as questionable and who see a real need for government to lessen its spending. Understanding this reality, rather than attempting to change the rhetoric to make spending more palatable, we may be better served by leaders who are willing to defend spending as more appropriate in the long-term than a failure to spend. If only our leaders who have been magnificent at convincing large majorities of us that spending on defense is essential, whatever the "cost," would step forward to argue similarly about education.

President Bill Clinton often describes public spending as "investment," and surely the beauty of given investments lies in the beholder. The danger of using terms like "investment" and "return" lies in the then necessary association of non-money entities (like education and children) with money terms. To do so invites those who disagree with a given "investment" to analyze the money "returns" as insufficient.

Among the problems with investments in education lies our inability to effectively analyze various districts and/or various programs in terms of money spent. There simply is too much outside influence upon learning that makes any real assessment of educational expenditures in terms of returns on the dollar largely valueless.

> It would be hard either to say how money should be spent on education to maximize the economic return or to defend some types of education policy that could follow from such an approach. The only really strong force for extra spending on education is parents' belief that it is good for their children, and parenthood is no longer analyzable as an investment activity. (Lloyd, 1994, p. 101)

If Trevor Lloyd is correct, then regardless of the difficulty of assessment, we need to concern ourselves with the tragedy of those in situations in which success, though not impossible, is prohibitively and increasingly difficult. If education spending cannot be easily analyzed in terms of dollar returns for dollar expenditures, perhaps we should focus on "doing the right thing" rather than making the proper investment. "Doing the right thing" can be either a good investment or a bad investment, but most often "doing the right thing" cannot be properly analyzed in dollar terms. To assume that more spending on education and a focus on improving the lives of those relegated to the bottom of our society will decrease later spending on welfare programs and prisons, while probably true, is nevertheless mostly theory. We as a society do not know which kids will turn out "right" and which will "stray." We have identified those we feel might be "at-risk," but even the wisdom of labeling people in such a manner is open to question. Since most of us are anecdotally armed with stories of kids who end up in prison even with all the educational advantages, and of other kids who end up as "highly valued and influential" citizens even without such benefits, it is nearly impossible to get beyond the rhetoric of anecdotes that act as "proof" for many people that their view is the correct view.

When Did We Abandon Education As a Way Up From Poverty?

Education used to be more vigorously represented in the political rhetoric as a panacea for poverty. While such hope is now less common, education for the poor is still an arena for confident pronouncements by many economists and business people, welfare specialists, and political and cultural entrepreneurs of various persuasions—"some of whom are startingly naive about the educational effects of what they propose" (Rosow & Zager, 1989, p. 126). Jerome M. Rosow and Robert Zager have been among those who have considered the way in which schools addressed poverty as an important test of an education system.

> Children from poor families are, generally speaking, the least successful by conventional measures and the hardest to teach by traditional methods. They are the least powerful of the schools' clients, the least able to enforce their claims or insist their needs be met, yet the most dependent on schools for their educational resources. (Rosow & Zager, 1989, p. 125)

Unfortunately, educators have not helped the cause, as many of our education "plans" have been little more than the rhetoric of the moment. Much of what has passed for "educational reform" has been articles and studies that, while often well-intentioned, have little practical application to the real world. Most are either attempts to confirm or refute the often asserted "liberal" approach, defined usually by "anti-liberals" as "throwing money at a problem." It is time to give up the liberal versus conservative fight and move on to more important battles.

Since there is the widely held view that modern school systems persistently do fail children in poverty, a sense of outrage runs through much educational writing about disadvantage. Several authors have recently added a note of urgency to this discussion. Gary Natriello, E.L. McDill, and Aaron M. Pallas (1990) give their survey of U.S. practice the subtitle, "Racing against Catastrophe." Jonathon Kozol's (1991) book, *Savage Inequalities*, presents an even bleaker portrait of willful neglect and deepening tragedy, while Jill E. Korbin (1992) speaks of the "devastation" of children in the United States. Part of the despair is a reaction to years of rightwing government, the stubbornly anti-reform policies of Presidents Reagan and George Bush, and what Robert Hughes (1993) saw as the Republicans' assimilation of racism with populism. "By 1989 about 44 percent of all black children lived below the poverty line, while the hopes for racial equality and greater educational opportunity for impoverished African Americans that had been raised in the mid 60s were all but extinct" (Hughes, 1993, p. 149).

How Did We Get Here? And Where Exactly is "Here?"

After the initial burst of educational reform programs in the early 1980s—in which fed-up politicians tried to legislate and regulate school improvements into existence—a period of slow reconsideration has been settling in, leading to the conclusion that deep and lasting reforms can only come about through the spontaneous efforts of individual teachers, schools, and districts. Unfortunately, the "spontaneous" efforts tended to focus upon a "slogan for reform." "Fixation on slogans diverts attention in this sense: argument becomes centered on the terms empowerment, school-based management, or restructuring, instead of on the central question of how to improve the performance of schools" (Rosow & Zager, 1989, p. 63).

It is unfortunate that the "slogan fixation" has been what a large part of "educational reform" has now become. This result (at least for now) has been the product of an evolutionary process which began in earnest with 1983's *A Nation at Risk* and has continued for the most part unabated ever since. John Murphy and Jeffry Schiller (1992) identified three prevailing explanations for our unsatisfactory performance: First, the quality of education in the schools is poor. Many of the advocates of this position argue that the quality of teaching is inadequate, that curriculum standards are low, that classes are too large, and that the instructional materials are inadequate for effective teaching and learning. Second, many students are coming to school as victims of intergenerational poverty, and, consequently, are not able to benefit from what schools have to offer. Third, many schools are reluctant to modify traditional delivery systems, which work with middle class students, to suit the needs of the disadvantaged, while maintaining standards.

Despite the merit of each theory, it is difficult to read the correct signs of the times to determine whether education is actually better or worse than it was in the past. Some say better, some say worse. Charles Willie and Inabeth Miller (1988) suspect that part of the problem in assessing the status of education is associated with the analytic perspective used (it all depends on where you stand). Their analysis centers upon the fact that the majority of the members of the National Commission on Excellence in Education were white and male. The National Commission declared that education in this nation is in a "current declining trend" (National Commission, 1983, p. 15). Yet the year the Commission's report was issued, more than 90 percent of all school-age children (including children of minority and majority populations) were matriculating students, and a majority of these students graduated from high school compared to earlier generations when most students dropped out.

Thus, a proper understanding of the assessment of education in the U.S. by the National Commission on Excellence in Education necessarily must consider the social locations of the prevailing number of its own members. They were not female nor from racial or ethnic minorities. The proportional participation of white males in education at all levels has declined as the proportional participation of others has increased. Thus, if one uses a self-centered analytic perspective, education in the United States could be interpreted to be in a declining state for white males but not for others (Willie & Miller, 1988).

The believed importance of school reform is characterized by the literature and the "certainty" of the rhetoric. The rhetoric of the 1980s and the early 1990s, which characterized our schools as being "at risk," has been reinforced with the belief (expressed in the form of a certainty) that if our schools cannot be reformed, our nation will not be able to maintain its leadership position in the world or be a place where the majority of citizens can be productive and self-fulfilled (Murphy & Schiller, 1992). It is not this author's position that we should not improve our schools and even "reform" them if need be, instead it is the intent of this chapter to caution the "buyers" of "reform proposals" to analyze not only the proposals but the "intent" of the reformers.

"Now That We Are Here, Should We Go Elsewhere?"

If we have learned anything since 1983, it is that the road to educational reform is paved with well-intended but limiting slogans and buzzwords. Phrases such as teacher empowerment, participation, school-based management, and the like are attractive, but putting those ideas into practice can as readily frustrate as advance the attainment of jointly desired goals. From a positive standpoint, these slogans have helped to mobilize teachers, whose sense of powerlessness has been pronounced in an educational system where decision-making authority is so heavily concentrated at the top. Buzzwords such as teacher professionalization and school restructuring have stimulated serious discussion about the problems that hamper teacher and local school initiatives for reform. "But the fixation on slogans also distracts attention from the central issue: how to improve schools" (Rosow & Zager, 1989, pp. 15-16).

David Perkins (1992) described educational reform initiatives as the "savior syndrome." Like other people in other circumstances, educators seem all the time to be looking for a savior.

> The savior syndrome label smacks of cynicism. It reveals a kind of impatience with the hunger for the quick fix, the deus ex machina that will put things right in the classroom. Education is a complex undertaking. The hope and eagerness with which the savior of the moment is greeted, assaulted, and all too often reduced to a trivialized version becomes tiresome. (Perkins, 1992, pp. 43-44)

"The problem with the syndrome is not with the candidates. Rather, the savior syndrome is symptomatic of one of the most misleading premises of educational reform: What we need is a new and better method" (Perkins, 1992, p. 44). "The reality is not that we need a better method, but that good teaching requires different methods for different occasions" (Perkins, 1992, p. 53). "Because differences are to be celebrated and not diminished, educational reform toward smart schools should be driven not by method but by curriculum—not by sophisticated visions of how to teach, valuable though they are, but by a broader, more ambitious vision of what we want to teach" (Perkins, 1992, p. 44).

"Schools Reflect Society—There's The Rub"

One of the great cliches that all young educators hear is that "schools reflect society." Since the truth of such a statement is seldom argued, the wonderment then lies in the uproar over "poor" schools and "bad" public education, and the subsequent blame placed upon the schools generally, and teachers particularly. If society is dumbing down, then why should we express surprise when our schools follow suit? What is critical for us as a society is to first recognize our limitations and then attempt to rise above them. When actors, athletes, and businesspeople are often our best-paid citizens, who needs higher education? Put less cynically, what is the expected "return" on studying hard and/or on spending dollars, both public and private, on educational pursuits? Derek Bok (1993) argued that "compensation policies in this country bear the mark of values that lie deep in our culture" (p. 248). So too, do the "compensation policies" that government leaders follow when funding various programs.

> By the 1980s the total cost of prenatal counseling, nutrition programs, family support, day care, parental leave, college loans, and all other methods of expanding opportunity had grown to formidable dimensions. When hard choices had to be made, therefore, many people who supported the current ideology were reluctant to spend heavily to open doors through new programs that brought so little direct benefit to themselves. It should hardly come as a surprise, therefore, that programs of this kind received little support throughout the 1980s. (Bok, 1993, p. 259)

Selling school improvement is not an easy task. Although many citizens decry the current condition of public schools and claim that they would like to see profound changes, there is likely to be opposition from many groups to any comprehensive improvement effort.

Among those most likely to express their opposition are: Those who believe that any new efforts would be expensive and likely to result in raising their taxes; Those who believe that the role of schools is to teach, and all of the social baggage that many students bring to the schools should not be treated by the schools; Those who believe that the best and the brightest will rise to the top and that vocational or other educational tracks should be available to all other students; Those who fear that school improvement activities will result in more heterogeneous classes thus allowing lower-ability-level youngsters to sit side by side with more able children and somehow taint them; Those school principals or teachers who understand that new school improvement activities are likely to require them to change their practices. (Murphy & Schiller, 1992, p. 257)

Previously this work described schools as a "battleground." Philosophers as acclaimed as Bertrand Russell have reminded us that "education has become part of the struggle for power" (1977, p. 145). In any power struggle there will be shifts and periods of time in which one group gains a temporary advantage, yet it is the nature of these times that any of the combatants on that battleground will not easily claim victory.

"If we cannot change our society from within our educational institutions then perhaps we can mandate change" (Rosow & Zager, 1989, p. 18). Such a mandated change in society would first require a reassessment of what we view as the "problems" at the core of our "decaying" culture and "virtues." If it is our people, be they ever less intelligent or ever less virtuous, then our solutions concerning more concern with teaching the "virtues," and a lessening of dependence upon government are probably good ones. If, instead our problems lie mostly within the circumstances in which many of our people find themselves both through their own "fault" and through the position granted to them by their birth, then a focus upon lessening some of the problems facing our "most dependent," such as poor educational opportunity, poverty, racism, and a lack of meaningful work opportunities might be a better approach.

> The transformation of schooling calls for bold new governmental initiatives. First among these must be to care for our impoverished pre-school children. Many of our public school system failures are directly related to problems that precede formal schooling, and unless we address these realities, we will continue our downward spiral. (Murphy & Schiller, p. 33)

"The Place For Teachers in Educational Reform"

Sara Lawrence Lightfoot writes harshly of the plight of teachers not treated with the respect due them: In the worst schools, teachers are demeaned and infantilized by administrators who view them as custodians, guardians, or uninspired technicians. In less grotesque settings, teachers are left alone with little adult interaction and minimal attention is given to their needs for support, rewards, and criticism. "The smart school, in contrast, honors the ingenuity, commitment, and centrality of teachers and provides time, resources, and encouragement toward the expansion and refinement of their craft" (Perkins, 1992, p. 223).

Regrettably, the "reform" debate spends too much time discussing "systemic reform" in the context of schools, while ignoring the need for "systemic reform" in the larger system that is our society. Another even more substantial "regret" is that policy discussions about education and poverty have frequently been conducted in the absence of the two groups most likely to understand the issues: poor people themselves, and the teachers in their schools. A striking example is the 1986 conference held by the U.S. Department of Education to reconsider Chapter I programs, which was entirely composed of academics, administrators, and policy analysts (Doyle & Cooper, 1988). Teachers have been expected to implement, but not create, policies, while poor people have been viewed as the objects of policy interventions rather than as the authors of social change.

Nearly everyone in the educational establishment accepts that reforms can be brought about only if teachers support them. Rosow and Zager (1989), among others, believe that whatever strategy is used to "reform" education, it remains critical that teachers' experiences and educational reasoning are at the center. The problem is that, by and large, those who direct the establishment believe teachers' support can either be purchased or commanded (Rosow & Zager, 1989). This belief is embedded in the organizational structure of most urban school districts. School districts, like all other management agencies, have three major functions: planning and design, implementation, and evaluation. Almost all planning and design is carried out by the local school boards and state governments, which set guidelines determining curriculum, resource allocation, personnel selection, school organization, and the many other details of school policy. For the most part, decision-making authority rests in the central office, while implementation is left to the individual schools, which have had little or no say in formulating those decisions or evaluating their outcome (Rosow & Zager, 1989).

The political nature of the operation of public schools is also a reason for the difficulty in enacting real reform. The school districts that govern our schools are creatures of the state. Whether they like it or not, school boards, state governors, and state legislators are charged with managing the public schools. This organizational structure undermines educational effectiveness and efficiency. First, it causes a lack of responsiveness to the variety of student needs and characteristics in different schools. District administrators have little or no day-to-day contact with students and teaching. The resulting standardization of textbook selection, curriculum, and evaluation criteria leaves little room for teacher discretion concerning these matters (Rosow & Zager, 1989). Second, teachers feel no responsibility or accountability for educational outcomes, since they have been excluded from decision making and evaluation. "Teachers view educational outcomes as resulting from factors beyond their control, a perspective that only reinforces an unwillingness to face actual student needs and a sense of powerlessness to change conditions" (Rosow & Zager, 1989, p. 30). But,

> ...substantive school improvement will require administrators to form partnerships with the teachers, in which the parties recognize their common interests and prevent their differences from blocking collaboration on educational reforms. (Rosow & Zager, 1989, p. 17)

We Have Met the Enemy, and the Enemy Is Us

Like many political wonderments, "reform" is now politically correct, whichever side you are on. The "Right" is commonly perceived to want educational reform through less teacher autonomy and more standardization. The "Left" is commonly perceived as seeking educational reform, too, only through greater teacher autonomy and less standardization. These accepted positions are, curiously, the opposite of the accepted positions of the "Right" and the "Left" in healthcare reform, as the "Right" wants little change and greatly fears a lessening of doctor autonomy, while the "Left" wants more radical change including more government involvement assuring universal coverage. The debate on educational reform, where often everything is nothing, mirrors the frequently changing stances of the left and the right who share only one common trait—inconsistency. The nature of reform in any area depends on the circumstances common only to that area, the persons doing the analyzing, and the political tides of the moment.

Chapter Four

A Rising Tide Lifts All Bores or Political "Virtue"

It's Not Whether You're Right or Wrong, It's How Persuasive You Are

The impact that William Bennett, Rush Limbaugh, G. Gordon Liddy, and others have had lies in the political pressures that their followers have put forth upon their elected leaders. Limbaugh, in particular, while not the first to put forth an agenda, is perhaps the best example of an influence that is able to persuade his followers to pressure Congress based mostly upon his word alone. Unlike Pat Robertson, who mostly claims to speak for and from God, Limbaugh manages to call his troops to action based on his views alone, which arguably at least, makes his influence even more impressive than that of those within the "Religious Right." While Limbaugh is not alone in his use of hyperbole and in his tendency to not allow contrary facts to stand in the way of a good message, he is a master of it, and as such is a master with such a devoted following that he is worthy of our attention.

Greed has been good, Limbaugh proclaims, because "a rising tide lifts all boats." In this instance the priming that has been done involved the thought that holds that since we *all* got richer in the 80s it could not possibly have been the decade of greed.

The facts indicate, however, that not *all* of us prospered or even incrementally moved ahead in the 1980s. Even scholars on the "Right" have conceded that the disparities between rich and poor actually grew during the 1980s. "During the 1980s the bucket of liberty and economic freedom rose, while the bucket of income equality fell. Upper-tier Americans significantly expanded their share of national wealth while low-income citizens lost ground, and Reagan policies were critical to this shift" (Phillips, 1990, p. 73). To what extent Limbaugh disagrees with the reality of the statistics that show increases in disparity or simply does not see increases in disparity as a problem is unclear, but it is quite clear that Limbaugh does not share the sentiment that the rich received any "breaks" during the 1980s or, apparently, any other period in American history.

Among Limbaugh's many observations that, if followed, present problems to the educational system is the following: "The poor in this country are the biggest piglets at the mother pig and her nipples. The poor feed off of the largesse of this government and they give nothing back. Nothing. They're the ones who get all the benefits in this country. They're the ones that are always pandered to" (Limbaugh, 1992, p. 40). Whether or not the "bounty" of the poor or the "suffering" of the rich is quite so extensive, Limbaugh's words, among others, have had a tremendous impact upon common perceptions of the poor in America. Our present preoccupation with "welfare reform" illustrates the depth of frustration that millions of Americans, and nearly all Limbaugh "dittoheads," feel toward government aid to the poor. The fact that "welfare" consumes and "wastes" less government money than do many other programs seems to be lost upon those consumed by "welfare reform." Broad-based governmental reform has become nearly synonomous with much narrower "welfare reform." These are not the "virtues" that all of us want imparted upon our children.

According to John Kenneth Galbraith (1992) it is actually social expenditure that favors the wealthy that is the most burdensome share of government spending. Accordingly, social security, medical care at higher income levels, farm income supports, financial guarantees to depositors in ill-fated savings and loans, and military spending are by far the largest part of the federal budget and that which under Presidents Ronald Reagan and George Bush showed by far the greatest increase (p. 26). What remains—expenditures for welfare, low-cost housing, health care for those otherwise unprotected, public education, and the diverse needs of the great urban slums, all comprising a significantly lesser share of total government spending—is what is perceived by Limbaugh and others as the "burden" of government.

Lewis H. Lapham (1993) uses a different approach to address the commonly accepted argument that the poor feed off the government by pointing out that when it comes to seeking help from the government, the poor merely share the traits of the non-poor. "The welfare client in hope of free housing or a free meal and the banker in hope of an investment credit or a tax break differ only in the class of their accommodations" (pp. 36-37). Janice Shields (1995) similarly addresses our obsession with welfare, pointing out that we have cut billions of dollars from housing, nutrition, and health, while remaining unscathed are billions in aid for dependent corporations. Shields cites the example of Lockheed Martin, a company that generates $11.6 billion in annual military sales.

> In a scenario of bizarre federal giveaways, U.S. taxpayers will spend $1 billion to cover the costs of plant shutdowns and employee relocations, even though 30,000 workers will lose their jobs. Another $31 million in federal money will go to top

officials of the company, one-third of their $92 million bonus package. (Shields, 1995, p. 5)

"Everyone is going to have to tighten their belts or the whole system will collapse in about forty years" (Limbaugh, 1992, p. 147). Whether the apocalypse is so near or not, what is most interesting is that the "everyone" Limbaugh refers to are the poor and those middle-class folks dependent upon social security income. Since, in this line of reasoning, taxes are inherently harmful and are disincentives for the rich to work and invest "harder," prudent policy conveniently limits this belt-tightening to the poor and lower middle-class. "Most government spending today doesn't go for services most people use. They are transfers of income from one person to another. In short, massive redistributions of wealth" (Limbaugh, p. 149). Galbraith, among others, would not argue that there have been massive redistributions of the wealth, but not as Limbaugh apparently thinks. Galbraith (1992), in fact, calls the statistics "decisive" (p. 105).

> The average after-tax annual income of those in the upper 20 percent of the income distribution increased in constant dollars from $73,700 in 1981 to $92,000 in 1990 (Testimony of Robert S. McNamara, former president of the World Bank before the Budget committee of the U. S. House of Representatives, July 30, 1991). The income of the average industrial worker declined in those same years. (Galbraith, 1992, p. 105)

The Implications of Polarization Upon Equity and Excellence

Beyond Galbraith's work, the increased polarization of society was further documented by Thomas Byrne Edsall (1984), who recognized an "extraordinary intensification of class voting" in the 1980s as compared with the previous two decades. For example, in 1956, President Dwight D. Eisenhower won by nearly the same margin in all income groups, but in 1980 Reagan won among the rich but was soundly beaten among those in the bottom 40 percent of income distribution. Barbara Ehrenreich (1990) makes the claim that "party affiliation became equally polarized, with the haves and have-nots having become solidly Republican and Democratic, respectively" (p. 206).

It is the ever-growing disparity in what Lapham (1993) called the "class of their accommodations" that troubles so many, and it is this disparity that so many worry will eventually result in the type of class warfare that will make "equal educational opportunity" even less credible than it is today. Many, including Galbraith (1992) and Robert Lekachman (1982), presented statistics supporting their views that the gap between the haves and have-nots widened dramatically during the Reagan-Bush years. Lapham (1993) made the following assertions:

> ...that all the numbers told the same dismal and undemocratic story: The income received by the richest one percent of American families improved by 49.8 percent in the years between 1977 and 1988; simultaneously, and by no means as a matter of chance, the income earned by families in the poorest one percent of the population declined by 14.8 percent. By 1991 it was no longer possible to pretend that everybody was as equal as everybody else. It was equally clear that the Reagan administration's several revisions of the tax laws sustained, often in great luxury, the American equivalent of a rentier class. (Lapham, 1993, p. 11).

In a most disturbing interview published late in 1981, David Stockman, the Director of the Office of Management and Budget and by far the most visible economic figure in the first Reagan Administration, said that the newly espoused doctrines were simply a serviceable cover story; the actual and deeper purpose was to lower taxes on the affluent (with William Greider, "Education of David Stockman," *The Atlantic*, December, 1981).

Lapham (1993), in writing about his perceptions of a small

"oligarchy," mused that "among the members of the oligarchy money has no discernible reality in the hands of lesser mortals because lesser mortals have no decent use for it" (p. 16). The fortunate few whom Limbaugh and other "Rightists" so ably represent somehow are able to earnestly preach that although money is good for the rich (hence no more tax disincentives) it is bad for the poor (throwing money at a problem). The accepted logic is that taxation is evil since the rich and relatively affluent need the incentive of good income as, if said more discreetly, the poor are deserving of their poverty.

The early years of the Reagan administration and the rise to power of the "New Right," as Ehrenreich (1989, p. 183) among others has referred to it, set the stage for those in powerful leadership positions to conveniently widen the gap between rich and poor. More startling than the thought that those among the privileged would seek such disparity is the ease with which it was sold to mainstream America.

Among the ideas adopted wholeheartedly by the new administration were the New Right's startling theories on poverty: it had been caused, strangely enough, by past efforts to cure it (Ehrenreich, 1989, p. 183). If the rhetoric and philosophy embraced by the Reagan team could be sold to the public (and even President Bill Clinton's rhetoric about "welfare reform" shows that it can and, in fact, was) then the burden of the middle class and the wealthy of "caring" for the poor could be lessened. The New Right's reasoning begins with the assumption that the poor are victims of a "culture" or a "syndrome" that disables people in the quest for upward mobility. This syndrome is seen as the product not of despair, but of the overly permissive welfare and anti-poverty programs championed by liberals (Ehrenreich, 1989, p. 185).

Since many of our leaders and our leading media figures, like Limbaugh, have convinced us that the welfare programs had "failed," the only rational thing for us to do is to eliminate these programs before they do us any more "harm." As natural primers, coupled with the significant fact that most of us aren't "poor," we welcomed the news that we had done all that we could, and that any more of our help would actually hurt by reaffirming that dreaded cycle of dependency and poverty.

Increased polarization and increased acceptance of that polarization has helped foster the argument that equity and excellence have been mutually exclusive, and our societal pendulum has swung too far toward equity and should be corrected by a shift towards excellence. Education stands at the forefront of social change, both real and perceived, and it is education that will ultimately bear the brunt of any political shifts that favor excellence at the cost of equity. The problem again becomes definitional, as the complex concepts of "equity" and "excellence" have been and can be interpreted differently by different people. Unfortunately, the concepts have come to be considered mutually exclusive, and any real improvement in both is seen as either unmanageable or altogether inappropriate.

"If It's Your Fault You're Poor, Then Get Off My Back"

It takes little imagination to extend this line of thought and to consider the burden such thought places upon education. If we have reasoned that helping the poor and unfortunate actually hurts them, it is not a great leap to see what impact such thought has had, and will continue to have, upon educational issues. Since schools reflect society and society's prevailing thought, it has become acceptable and somewhat popular to hold the view that using money to try to help shore up "bad" schools would only hurt them by making them more dependent, and thus less likely to show initiative. From such thought freely flow theories that emphasize "excellence."

One example of this is the theory espousing that improvement of the public schools can be had by giving parents vouchers to use at private schools, under the assumption that increased competition and voucher systems for all parents, regardless of need, would allow "anyone" the ability to choose a better school. Social Darwinism run amok. Inherent in the theory of social Darwinism is the knowledge that "improvement of the breed will necessarily be difficult for the weak and sickly."

Those extolling many of the "excellence in education" proposals rest assured that their own children and their own children's friends are not among the "weak and sickly." Such proposals are attempts to abandon the concept of "equity" in favor of the concept of "excellence." To pursue "excellence" with such vigor, while limiting our concern for "equity," fails to recognize the terms as vague and complex concepts.

> The democratic truth in equalization is that all children should learn enough to be able to live not only a minimally decent life, but also to participate effectively in the democratic process. A democratic state, therefore, must take steps to avoid those inequalities that deprive children of educational attainment adequate to participate in the political processes. (Gutmann, 1987, p. 134)

Reagan's rhetoric, like that of Bush and Limbaugh, included eliminating "quotas" and "government waste," which not so coincidentally prevented people of color and ordinary salary from sharing equally in opportunity. "Such rhetoric and subsequent aid in enforcement reductions had the effect of reducing a democratizing statistic that had steadily risen throughout America's history—the proportion of children entering colleges whose parents had never attended one" (Reeves, 1985, p. 123). Implicit within that decline in participation is the logical extension of a lessening of the value of education in a society that seeks less "equalization" and more "excellence." The preference for "excellence" at the expense of "equity" has permeated the culture of not only the Reagan and Bush administrations, but through mouthpieces like Limbaugh these preferences have been allowed to permeate aspects of our culture heretofore the province of more reasonable, if itself flawed, debate.

The decisions made that impact public education are decisions that take years to analyze and, if wrongly made, years to correct, sometimes to the detriment of an entire generation. These decisions also effect any democraticizing element of public education and follow the concern expressed by many about the increasing economic polarity of our society. "The decisions we make concerning public education in this country could make the difference between reestablishing the United States as the land of opportunity and becoming even more decisively a land of haves and have-nots" (Grieder, 1992, p. 73). Journalists, like William Grieder, are not alone in their expressions of the increasing "duality" of our society. Political leaders such as President Jimmy Carter have also expressed their concern:

> Our country's history tends to move in cycles, and today we have come to another turning point, as the segregation of our society has become almost as insidious as it was thirty years ago. The division is between rich and poor, but still largely along racial lines. There are now two Americas. Those of us who live in the affluent and comfortable America have homes, jobs, education, healthcare, and convenient services, while many of our neighbors down the road don't have these things. (Carter, 1992, p. 194)

As fewer families have children in the public schools, there will likely be continuing threats to the economic advancement of schools. The unfortunate, if understandable, tendency exists in our society to seek more government services that directly benefit us while simultaneously deploring programs that benefit others. Robert J. Samuelson (1994) refers to it as the "popular inconsistency" in which Americans are "hopelessly dependent on Big Government and rabidly contemptuous of it" (p. 45). This political reality, coupled with the widespread inability or unwillingness to delve deeply into long term results of given actions, will likely mean a continuation of widespread unwillingness to spend money on "not directly beneficial" public schools.

"Popular Inconsistency, Part II"

Another disturbing inconsistency fostered by the best primers has been the ease with which many mainstream Americans have been sold on the evils of government spending on the poor and working classes, and the simultaneous wisdom of allowing government spending on those of privilege. We have societally failed to look deeply into the rather mundane issue of public expenditures, and we have thereby allowed those of privilege to escape vigourous public scrutiny. After all, we really don't understand or appreciate the flow of millions of dollars to various contractors or the economic effects of taxation abatements and incentives. At the same time, however, we tend to completely understand and thereby scrutenize what the "poor" take home from the grocery store. Limbaugh vividly represents the inconsistency of thought that both deplores and admires "socialistic" programs, depending primarily upon the targeted beneficiaries. According to Limbaugh, the "socialism" that is welfare, public education, and the like is clearly bad. Like a good true-believer, Limbaugh agreed with Reagan about the merits of capitalism, and the demerits of socialism. In one of his earliest and most frequently quoted observations upon becoming President, Reagan said that "in the U. S., government was not the solution to problems, it was the problem." He proceeded to attack that "problem" by allowing an unprecedented expansion of government.

Since it likely would have been politically fatal to attack social security, old-age pensions, or publicly-supported health care (see Bill and Hillary Clinton), Reagan (and Bush) didn't.

Support to farm income was equally favored, as was the government rescue of failing financial institutions and therewith those who have entrusted their money thereto. Socialism is deeply abhorrent except for those for whom it is financially "necessary." Other "socialist" tendencies within our society, such as allowing corporate tax breaks and financial "incentives" to relocating companies, or in allowing similar incentives to wealthy developers in order to stimulate the economy by erecting large commercial developments, are seen as perfectly acceptable. The inconsistency of condemning "government handouts" to poor and working people while lauding "incentive packages" and "tax breaks" that accrue to millionaire developers is nothing short of remarkable. The fact that much of the public does not see the inconsistency is nothing short of amazing.

The excesses of the 1980s must be considered brilliant short-term policy by those who "won." "Deregulation was widely favored and remarkably publicly well-accepted. Where deregulation could yield short-term profits, it was considered a worthy goal. The savings and loan fiasco is one dramatic consequence" (Chomsky, 1991, p. 83). The taxpayer was called upon to "bail out" the speculators who had hoped to profit from savings and loan deregulation. Neil Bush, while not the largest offender, is perhaps the most "in our face" example of the power of money and influence during this period. In becoming a director of Silverado, despite his youth and inexperience, he was allowed to use government money to wildly speculate. Had all gone well, and the real estate market not fallen, he could perhaps be another shining symbol of prosperity and unabashed capitalism. As it was, however, he became a virtual recluse in 1992, rather than his father's most visible campaigner. One wonders if he intended to pay society back, had great success occurred, in the same manner that society must bear his burden of failure. The Neil Bush story is merely an anecdote, a gross oversimplification of the era, nevertheless he stands as a very visible reminder of what we valued in the 1980s, wealth and capitalism, at the expense of more long-term investments such as education. More to the point, we valued "excellence" in our society, not "equity."

Poor persons have no monopoly on laziness, as rich persons have no monopoly on industriousness. To begin to believe otherwise becomes not only a sad prejudice but dangerous public policy. To insist that those less "successful" have therefore worked less hard and with less perseverance is precisely the "intolerance" that is the most troubling aspect of the Limbaugh phenomenon specifically, and the practice of priming generally. Americans show widespread support for some of these beliefs. A 1980 survey by James R. Kluegel and Eliot R. Smith reported that despite years of media coverage indicating that American poverty is often a result of involuntary unemployment, substandard wages, medical emergencies, family crises, or other circumstances beyond one's control, most Americans believe that individuals are responsible for their wealth or lack of wealth. Not surprisingly, the wealthier one tends to be—from whatever source, true industriousness, luck, or even inheritance—the more one tends to believe in the "individualism" doctrine espousing personal responsibility.

Limbaugh, and to a lesser extent Bennett, no doubt, want what is best for America, as they see "America." The trouble is, their America, where the rich work hard and toil under too much government regulation and too much tax disincentive, and where the poor lazily collect their government bounty, is worlds apart from the real America. While many of these persons preach their "altruistic" concerns for America, they continue to advance agendas that promote their own self-interests. David C. Berliner and Bruce J. Biddle (1995) put it best:

> ...rich and powerful people often create marvelous explanations for why they should continue to enjoy their privileges. Consider, for example, the many creative rationales offered by the tobacco industry for discounting or hiding research that

links smoking with cancer, or the huge panoply of "disinter-
ested" objections to national health care voiced by rich doctors,
drug companies, and insurance executives. Such statements
are obvious masks for self-interest. It seems at least possible
that similar self-interest may have also motivated some recent
actions of the critics of education. (p. 149)

To listen to Limbaugh and begin to believe that the people
who work hard in difficult jobs could get further ahead without
government intervention if they just weren't so lazy, is to listen
to the rantings of someone who has gotten ahead without the
burden of heavy lifting and with the support of family. Not all are
so fortunate, and it should be recognized that political aims such
as universal health care, greater aid to the public schools that
face and have to deal with the most severe societal problems, and
more progressive taxation should not be derailed by public
support for the affluent minority, like Limbaugh, who simply do
not want any changes that might somehow affect their rather
contented lives. Until the contented work 40 plus hours a week
in a factory or packing house, or even behind the counter at
McDonalds, and find that they are just marginally making ends
meet, their credibility in knowing what is best for those that do
is suspect at best.

As educators we need to "warn" not of the danger of any
particular person, but of the danger of priming, and the intolerance that is fostered through the blind acceptance of the leader's
decries, whether that leader is from the Right or the Left. The
teaching of "cynicism," more than "virtues," should be viewed
quite positively in our democracy where informed and uninformed voters make significant decisions. It is far more cynical
to allow a growing atmosphere to exist wherein persons are
"informed" by the opinions of others, rather than by information-
assisted interpretation of the issues themselves.

Transfer of resources to the rich, partial dismantling of the
limited welfare system, an attack on unions and real wages, and

expansion of the public subsidy for high-technology industry through the Pentagon system were seen by Noam Chomsky (1991), among others, as the lasting legacies of the Reagan administration. All of these have had a direct impact upon American public education. As the federal deficit increased yearly, adding to the increasing and newfound federal debt, efforts to "lessen" government gained wheels. The United States had quickly gone from the world's leading creditor nation to the world's leading debtor (Chomsky, 1991, p. 82). In order to begin to concentrate upon the mounting debt, something not even considered by Reagan, his successors would have to attempt to cut back on federal spending. Among those programs that are now going to be "under attack" for many years are any programs that increase expenditures involving such "indirect benefits" as education.

As educational policy is undeniably related to politics, politics is undeniably all about money. Annual budget traumas at all levels of government register the agonizing process of distributing among many claimants the community's output of necessary and desirable goods and services (Lekachman, 1992). "How the politicians allocate money shapes the fortunes of young and old; the poor, the middle class, and the genuinely affluent" (Lekachman, 1992, p. 21). The Reagan and Bush legacy will be lasting. It will take years to correct some of the excesses, and years to restore more fairness to our tax code. Consequently, those who always had the options within our society now have even more and better options. Those who seldom had options now have even less palatable ones. These tremendous disparities between rich and poor make for an environment in which those at the top who control more and more wealth have little real stake in America's public educational system.

The Constitution did not "burden" the federal government with the role of educating its youth, and the federal government has accordingly not been, in relative terms, a great source of money for our public schools. Under Reagan, from 1981 to 1989, the federal government dropped its share of support for public education from 9.2 percent to 6.2 percent. The loss of revenue was, of course, felt by local schools, but the importance of the loss was even greater in the symbolic message it sent. "Less government" was the theme. The reality, of course, has been more government, but not in areas seen as unimportant, such as public schooling. Education is too important to be considered as a mere segment of the budget, and too important to continually face the threat of downsizing as if it were like the defense budget, where spending could increase or decrease depending on outside threats. The "threat" to national security from downsizing public education lies within the United States. Every child who feels "devalued" becomes an adult who may very well feel no value for his or her life and well-being, and consequently perceive of others as having little to no value as well.

The diminishment of class as a meaningful dimension of "humanness" and the abolition of the steep gradients of wealth and poverty, and power and helplessness, would allow for the advent of true and genuine democracy (Ehrenreich, 1989). By emphasizing services such as education that improve the lives of everyone and widen the opportunities for those in need, we will approach the level playing field that should aid all of us, rich and poor, in feeling better about ourselves and our opportunities for advancement. Legislators, whether national, state, or local, almost always speak of their dedication to education. Their true values as represented by their votes and positions toward appropriations, however, more clearly define them. It is this author's hope that a greater recognition of long-term results, through a more careful analysis of the options, will lead to greater emphasis on education in reality and not simply in the public rhetoric. It's time to be truthful, and either devalue education in our words to more properly reflect our deeds, or to actually treat education as kindly in our deeds as we so ably do in our words.

Chapter Five

Is "Virtue" a Conservative or Liberal Trait

"When Did Myth Become Reality and Reality Become Myth: It's Not the Economy, Stupid, It's Public Perception"

A "virtue" treatise would not be complete without reference to President Bill Clinton; Rush Limbaugh's and William Bennett's answer to the question of whether the apocalypse is upon us. Even the President's ardent supporters seldom hold him up as a "paragon" of virtue, and in fact, as critics have contended, a Clinton strategy has been to downplay the importance of personal "character" and emphasize the "business of running the government."

"Character," however vaguely and fluidly defined, divided the electorate in 1996 as it had in 1992. According to Robert B. Smith (1997), those

> ...more concerned about character voted for Bush, were Republicans, and were conservatives. Homemakers and housewives were more concerned about character than were employed

women. Those not paid for their work—homemakers, house-wives, students, the retired, the unemployed—were more concerned than the employed. Voters less concerned about character supported governmental interventions for equity, equality, and health. (p. 17)

Does this mean that in order to have real "character" one must oppose equity, equality, and health? Or does it merely mean that one must oppose greater governmental involvement into these areas? Still, if by opposing government intervention, one effectively must know that equity, equality, and health are not going to improve; isn't such a person less than "virtuous?" While I don't claim to know, it does seem at least open to debate that lessening government "interference" into the lives of our citizens who might benefit from such "interference" is much more a cheap and selfish "cop-out," and much less the acts of those of genuine character and virtue.

Whatever the definition of genuine "character," the President, as our most "public" of public figures, is certainly a lightning rod for our many interpretations of character. Robert E. Denton, Jr. (1988) viewed the presidency as "primarily and essentially a rhetorical institution. It is defined by public communication and functions through communication in a variety of ways and con-texts" (p. xiv). The perceptions that a president engenders within the public are vital to that president's political survival.

Paul Brace and Barbara Hinckley (1992) cite the Reagan administration as evidence that public perceptions can be shaped and adjusted. "Ronald Reagan convinced people they were better off than they had been four years before, even if objective circumstances did not merit this conclusion" (p. 27). The belief that, in politics, style often triumphs over substance, is no longer news either inside or outside of the beltway. It seems beyond debate that, in our mass media age, we have become collectively accustomed to the importance of "style" in politics, especially presidential politics.

President Clinton, like Reagan, is a skilled orator who, seemingly at least, is able to convince people of things that less skilled orators cannot. If the Presidency is, in fact, largely a rhetorical institution, requiring skills in rhetoric to "succeed," then Clinton and Reagan certainly support such a thesis. One need only consider the period since 1980 and compare the rhetorical skills of reelected Presidents Reagan and Clinton with one-term Presidents Jimmy Carter and George Bush to consider the value of rhetoric.

President Clinton's first term seems to be divided rather sharply into a meandering, ambitious, and largely disastrous (politically) first three years, followed by a focused and largely successful fourth year. This chapter, among other things, looks back at the first three years of Clinton's presidency by way of contrast with his fourth year in office. Clinton's first three years were characterized by rather widespread disapproval, largely as a result, in this author's view, of three things: first, he failed to receive proper credit for the good things he managed to do; second, selective perception by many within the electorate seemed to have coincided with Clinton's first three years; and third, Clinton was the victim of massive "priming" of the public by Limbaugh and others.

The remarkable aspect of these three years is illustrated by the disparity between his actions in office and the perceptions of those actions as held by many voters. A large percentage of the American people failed to see the reality of the results of the President's first three years in office, instead having clung to myths that had been carefully and skillfully cultivated by the President's most ardent detractors. Many reasons combined to allow such mythmaking a fertile ground, and any one reason is likely to be a vast oversimplification. With that in mind, this chapter attempts to look at some of the factors that led to the overwhelming Republican victory in November 1994, and its sharp contrast with both the elections of 1992 and 1996. Doing so requires an analysis of some of the many "selective perception" problems that faced the Clinton administration in 1994, within the context of widespread "reality avoidance" and "myth acceptance."

The 1994 mid-term elections that resulted in an overwhelming Republican Party victory and an equally overwhelming Democratic Party defeat had been marked by many as the beginning of the end of Clinton's Presidency. Since that lowpoint, Clinton has been remarkably able to revive his political fortunes. This chapter examines why such a lowpoint occurred, despite the fairly widespread successes of his administration. Whether the onset of "virtue" as a concern had anything to do with Clinton's fall from grace is highly debatable, still there does seem to be a correlation between the rise of the "Right" and the "Right's" control of the "virtue" debate. The Right's adoption of virtue as their exclusive domain is but one aspect of their victory in 1994. Recognizing the importance of controlling "virtue" does not diminish the necessary understanding that many other factors—economically, sociologically, politically, culturally, etc—surely played equal, if not larger, roles in the election of 1994.

The desire for change that brought Clinton the presidency was thought by many to be the result of mass disillusionment among the American public, which created a favorable climate for the candidate of "change." By the end of the campaign in 1992, the three major candidates, Bush, Ross Perot, and Clinton, all characterized themselves as the appropriate agent of change. The significance of the candidates' recognition of the need for "change" was perhaps best articulated by the candidacy of Bush, the incumbant President, who essentially campaigned that his next four years would be different from his first.

> By 1992, three decades of evidence that U.S. politics and government didn't work—from Lyndon Johnson and Vietnam, Richard Nixon and Watergate, through endless petty congressional scandals to George Bush and a blind presidency de-

feated by a recession it couldn't understand—had brought Americans to the brink of mass disillusionment. (Phillips, 1994, p. 5)

The disillusionment that was so prevalent in 1992 did not bode well for the incumbant President, and had, by November of 1994, been revised by able conservatives and even moderates so that many within the electorate seemed to believe that the disillusionment felt in 1992 was a mistake, and the rejection of government as it stood in the 1980s was wrong. Persons who voted to change things in 1992 had, by 1994, seemingly wanted a return to "the good old days."

Bob Dole's 1996 Presidential campaign also reflected his belief that voters wanted to return to the good old days of supply side economics as avidly preached by his running mate, Jack Kemp. Despite what seem to be contradictions between Dole's lengthy political career and his newfound devotion to supply side economics, his unabashed enthusiasm for the concept illustrated his belief that returning to the "good old days" was the way to win the election. The contradictions between Dole's prior record and his newly found "need" to cut taxes across the board, while seen by many as merely an electioneering ploy, were seldom, if ever, seen as evidence of a "shady character." This chapter addresses the concepts of "selective perceptions" and revisits the concept of "priming"—two concepts that have created an environment in which many of those still clamoring for "change" seem to have vastly different understandings of what they believe Clinton has or has not done, and the reality of the genuine change that Clinton has overseen.

The combination of selective perception on the part of many within the electorate, and the mass-revisionist history that has made "longing for the good old days" rather prevalent within our society, were ominous signs pointing toward the end of Clinton's political future. Somewhere in the period between November of 1992 and November of 1994, a large percentage of voting Americans began to believe that the 1980s were significantly better than they actually were, while simultaneously believing that the period between 1992 and 1994 was much worse than it actually was. Apparently, just as our individual perceptions of vacations tend to get better the longer in the past that they have occurred, our society has largely bought into the myths of prosperity that were the 1980s and abandoned the reality of a growing economy and deficit reduction that was the period between 1992 and 1994.

While it is always worthy of analysis when a president is unpopular because of failed policy, it is even more interesting when a president is unpopular less for the reality of his programs and policy than for his *perceived* failures in policy. A serious analysis of the Clinton administration seems to lead one to conclude that, for better or worse, Clinton has altered prior policy nearly as radically as did Reagan, who arguably enacted more change than any prior administration since the days of Franklin Delano Roosevelt. Charles O. Jones (1996) addresses the logistical problem of transforming from the relatively easily accomplished "candidate of change" to the much harder "agent of change." "The separated system is not well designed to produce major changes in a short time" (p. 18). Further "whereas change was a dominant theme in the 1992 campaign, the election results did not produce a clear mandate for the winner" (p. 19).

More importantly, and eminently more interesting, has been the "selective perception" of large segments of the American public in analyzing presidential performance. Despite the obvious fact that perceptions can be shaped and adjusted over time, the early years of Clinton's Presidency were severely hampered by large segments of the public's "selective perceptions." Dislike for President Clinton ran so deep for large numbers of people that even when he did something they seemingly might like, they either failed to notice it, or perhaps most remarkably, they actually gave the credit to someone else. It was Clinton's inability, in his first three years, to reshape these selective perceptions that proved to be his greatest obstacle to success in the court of public opinion.

The perceptions surrounding the Clinton Presidency have, like most, been shaped and adjusted, and therefore, although it may be too early to consider the Clinton presidency either "failed" or "successful," it is not too early to examine the remarkable shift in the political winds that allowed David Letterman and Jay Leno to seemingly overnight change their punchlines from Clinton's "one-term presidency" to the "futility of Dole's campaign against him." Unforeseen events such as the tragic Oklahoma City bombing in April 1995 which buoyed Presidential approval ratings is ample evidence that "things can change," and that political winds can shift. These winds radically shifted back and forth and back again between November of 1992 and November of 1996. As the 1996 election neared, and polls indicated that a possible "landslide" in favor of Clinton was in the works, it was interesting to note, as did Jones (1996), that each of our previous post-Second World War Presidents reelected (Dwight Eisenhower, Richard Nixon, and Reagan) were also reelected in a landslide.

It is not too early to consider the impact that communication, both true and untrue, has had upon the "revised" history, particularly that of the period of November 1992 to November 1994. The role the "media" plays in shaping popular opinion is open to debate, and depending upon which side one lines up on, the media can often be either too "liberal" or too "conservative." In this age of the lessening influence of "mainstream" media and the increasing influence of opinion or "talk" radio and television, there has been a distinct change in the nature of what "news" is now reported to the public.

Unfortunately for President Clinton, much of the "news" that talk radio reports is blatantly untrue, and nearly all the "news" from these same sources is more objectively seen less as news and more as "anti-Clinton rhetoric." It seems that Clinton's fourth year returned him to his campaign style of leadership that so effectively allowed him to capture the Presidency. Jones (1996) described Clinton's Presidency as the completion of the transition to a "campaign style of governing." We know from public opinion that it took until Clinton's fourth year for his "campaign style of governing," in which he was more combative toward his foes and more forceful in his rhetoric, to begin to resonate with the American electorate.

Beyond any impact that misperceptions may have on any one election lies the impact that such misperceptions have upon policy and also the impact such misperceptions have had upon the entire course of the Clinton presidency. Clinton's popularity early in his Presidency, while not as important as in November of 1996, was still a significant factor that controlled much of what he could accomplish. His popularity, therefore, determined much of the success or failure that his opponents and he will both attribute to his presidency. His popularity also determines, to some extent at least, how willingly members of Congress follow his lead. Ever accountable to the voting public, congresspersons, particularly biannually-elected representatives, are reluctant to be seen supporting an unpopular position and/or an unpopular President. Democratic candidates did not always welcome Clinton, and in some states they wouldn't even appear with the President (Jones, 1996). "Presidents no longer govern for four years based on the strength of one election; today the electoral mandate is continually updated and reviewed by public-opinion polls" (Brace & Hinckley, 1992, p. 18).

"The Good Old Days of 1992"

Many in our society worry about "revisionist" historians who attempt to influence our reading of history rather than simply reporting it. This author submits that it isn't only historians who can revise the past, it is the American public as fed by its representatives and influential public figures as well. It is the prevalence of such a mass-revisionist culture that once seemed to mandate the end of Clinton's presidency after four years, despite its successes, in order to return to the more accepted passive leadership style of someone more like President Reagan, someone less concerned with (if also less able to master) the details, and more focused on a simple (if impossible) agenda for the future. It is likely these perceptions (as well as his knowedge and experience within the inner-workings of Washington) that transformed deficit-hawk Dole into Reagan revisited, a man who promised to simultaneously cut our taxes, raise our benefits, grow the economy, improve our schools, fight our crime, and generally make us proud to be Americans again.

This person may also be someone with the same character flaws as have haunted Clinton, but who will manage to somehow convince a majority, or perhaps merely a plurality of us, that those same character flaws that have blinded many to the achievements of Clinton's presidency are not relevant to his own and our own lives. The issue of character itself is endlessly interesting, as our concern with it shifts radically from time to time. In 1980 and 1984, Republicans were preaching the gospel that an affable and rather "disengaged" man could make a great president. Republicans wanted people to judge their leader by his accomplishments and ideas, not his attention to details; but by 1992 Republicans urged Americans to forget about ideas or the lack of them (the "vision thing") and instead focus on Bush's "likeability" and "trust" factors (Frum, 1994).

With so much focus upon public opinion polls that reflect short-term reaction to immediate problems, real or perceived, it is difficult for a President and his handlers to ignore the steamrolling effect of public opinion that is up to the minute. Our societal focus on the up-to-the-minute popularity ratings of a president seems to betray and downplay the more significant fact that the impact of presidential policies can last for generations. Long-term thought seems more and more to be lost upon an American public and an American press more than happy to placate that public.

"Enough About the Myth, What About the Reality"

"The press has endlessly covered communication, character, tone, style, and running shorts. Now how about a look at the record?" (Alter, 1994a, p. 49). It is the press, often referred to mostly by "non-liberals" as the "liberal press," that has been so reluctant to focus upon Clinton's record, to his eternal detriment. The interesting aspect of the press coverage is the myth of the perceived and widely cited "liberal bias." It is that myth that has enabled conservatives to escape criticism by a shrug and a reference to the "liberal press." In contrast, liberals and moderates are often left more open to "valid" criticism because they are not up against the "liberal bias" which is perceived by many as clouding a journalist's questioning.

Consequently, "non-conservatives" are in the unenviable position of having to defend themselves against "tough" reporting, while conservatives must only defend themselves against "biased" reporting. Given this environment, much of what ailed Clinton early on in his Presidency was his failure to communicate his message to the people through this media, "liberal" or not, but an even greater failure has come in his inability to use the press more effectively in an effort to overcome the "selective perceptions" of many voters.

"It's More Than Meets the Press, However"

President Clinton can take some solace in the fact that his high disapproval ratings during the first three-quarters of his first term were due less to real presidential failings than to perceived failings. Whatever factor Perot had in the 1992 election, it cannot be disputed that Clinton won the presidency with a mere 43 percent of the vote. Clinton had, as described by Jones (1996), an ambitious agenda but no mandate. As of his inauguration, 57 percent of the voters disapproved of Clinton (or at least approved more of someone else). During the first three years of his term, a large and increasingly militant number of those 57 percent grew in their opposition daily regardless of what Clinton did or did not do.

The importance of myth, and the subsequent diminishment in the value of reality, is what made and makes Clinton most vulnerable. The perception (valid or not) that is permeating much of the country's mainstream press and therefore mainstream perceptions, is that of a country on the brink of disaster unless we diminish the responsibility of a government that is obviously not up to the task. The validity of such a thesis is debatable, but it is interesting to note that those who stand most united against big government while simultaneously placing the blame on the "decay" of our society, our sliding culture, and our lost "values," are those who are quite contented with the present state of their lives. These people feel little need for government intervention into healthcare, and even less need for increased taxes to support other government programs. "Conservatives focus on the culture-is-responsible thesis in order to enable them to sidestep the speculative bubble of the 1980s and to insist that Reaganomics worked, so further tax cuts on the wealthy and further deregulation should be renewed with vigor, not abandoned in the 1990s" (Phillips, 1994).

> Republicans, collectively, are simply not free to admit that serious economic declines—for the middle class and the American dream, in accelerating national indebtedness, and the eroded competitiveness of key industries—occurred during the Reagan-Bush period. Party economic policies are too closely linked to the interests that profited from the recent

era's speculative bubble, tax cuts, bailouts, and trade liberal-
izations. (Phillips, 1994, p. 64)

Americans in 1992 were beginning to believe that the excesses of the 1980s were in fact bad policy. By 1994, however, a
year in which even a disgraced former President was lauded
heroically in death, Americans began to mass-produce revisionist history. By the 1994 mid-term elections, many Americans
believed that the reality of deficit reduction was a myth and the
myth of higher taxes on the middle and lower classes was a
reality. A society in which Limbaugh controlled much of the
debate and even received an occasional response from the President himself, was a society that was ripe for mythmaking and
that was subject to revisionist history on an unprecedented
scale.

Ben Wattenberg (1995) skewers "liberals" and "liberalism"
but never actually explains what distinguishes a liberal from a
conservative. Bert A. Rockman (1996) distinguishes between
Democrats who "want to do things," and Republicans who "more
often want to stop things" (p. 357). He asserts that it is much
simpler to stop things than to do things. Hence, "successes"
politically are actually "easier" for Republicans than for Democrats. David P. Barash (1992) distinguishes (no doubt overbroadly)
liberals and conservatives thusly: "liberals feel that the poor, the
disenfranchised, must be protected. Conservatives feel that the
rich must be protected, from the potential political power of an
envious and good-for-nothing majority" (p. 23). However grand
this overstatement, it does seem that today's hot issue of "welfare
reform" is all about protecting us taxpayers from a "good-for-
nothing" segment of the population. Joel F. Handler (1994)
writes of our societal "obsession" with welfare reform, in the
world of "symbolic politics" (p. 43):

> The majoritarian society affirms its norms by stigmatizing
> others. This is a grave characteristic, primarily because it
> seems so ubiquitous and so enduring. AFDC recipients are

still characterized as primarily African American, sexually promiscuous, "underclass," criminal, drug users who are spawning a new generation of criminals. One wonders whether attitudes will ever change. We realize the cruelty of these stereotypes when we examine who these people often actually are: single adults trying to get off welfare, raise their children, and make lives for themselves and their children. They are the Willie Hortons of the nineties. (Handler, 1994, p. 43)

Those proclaiming "virtue" and "character" seem to do so best when they stigmatize others. Recognizing "virtue" by proclaiming oneself virtuous and those unlike you as lacking in virtue, while seemingly effective, is simplistic, condescending, and elitist beyond compare, yet we seem to congratulate those that do so with tremendous book sales and injections of credibility that far surpass any that might be earned.

Theodore C. Sorenson (1996), in my view, put it best:

> I do not believe that either of this country's two major political parties has a monopoly on truth, patriotism, or virtue.... Both parties include scoundrels and weaklings within their ranks as well as dedicated public servants. Both parties cater excessively to big campaign contributors and local pork-barrel projects. (pp. 4-5)

Democrats as defenders of the "welfare state" have been largely unable to deal effectively with the rhetoric of the Right that has chained the welfare albatross around the neck of the Democratic Party, much like Willie Horton was chained to Michael Dukakis. However unfair and invalid these perceptions are, their validity as effective political tools has been illustrated by Clinton's pledge to "end welfare as we know it," and his support of such a bill despite grave misgivings of many influential Democrats. The lessons of Dukakis had seemingly not been lost upon Clinton, who would not have the "welfare albatross" hung around his neck.

Perceptions have held that "liberals" focus upon raising the poor, while conservatives focus upon seeing to it that the non-poor don't fall. However worthwhile if may be for society to both "raise the poor" and "keep the wealthy from falling," it has been the mainstay of political rhetoric during our recent history to polarize both parties as caring only for one or the other of society's "halves."

Marian Wright Edelman (1992) writes:

> Somehow we are going to have to develop a concept of enough for those at the top and at the bottom so that the necessities of the many are not sacrificed for the luxuries of the few. I do not begrudge billionaires or millionaires their incomes as long as children's basic needs of food and health and shelter and child care and education are met. But something's out of balance when the number of millionaires in the 1980s almost doubled and the number of poor children increased by three million—almost 30 percent—and children and the poor still face a vastly uneven playing field in the budget process compared with the military and the wealthy. Every dollar for domestic and poor children's program spending requires a huge fight, while the military trough seems bottomless, even as Communism is crumbling worldwide and violence and child abuse and neglect and poverty and joblessness are epidemic nationwide. (pp. 50-51)

"It's Perceptions About the Economy, Stupid"

Unlike Clinton's campaign managers in his quest for presidential office, who constantly reminded themselves and their boss that "it's the economy stupid," students of elections have needed little reminding that the focus of elections is the economy. "Incumbent parties almost always keep the White House if inflation is moderate and the unemployment rate is falling in the year leading up to the election" (Krugman, 1990, p. 1). "Probably no other guide to presidential fortunes has attracted more intense scholarly scrutiny" (Haller & Norpoth, 1994, p. 625).

Consumers, in their role as voters, "inflict electoral pain upon elected officials who are unable to meet their expectations" (Haller & Norpoth, 1994, p. 648).

Although the expectations are often flawed, and the rational basis for the expectations themselves is sometimes severely flawed, living up to or down to the expectations of the voters is crucial. Despite the importance of the economy upon presidential performance and upon the chances of presidential "success," many within the Clinton administration, including President Clinton himself, are quick to point out that many of his initial difficulties can be attributed in part to his unusually ambitious and controversial program and to the tendency of the media to occupy themselves more with the mechanics of presidential performance than on the substance of presidential programs (Greenstein, 1994).

Whatever the focus, there have been substantive Clinton "economic" victories. One such victory has been the reform of defense procurement procedures so that quartermasters can now go to their local discount store to buy hammers and other simple tools and thus avoid the paperwork, and other bureaucratic intrusions, that can result in the "necessity" of ordering $700 toilet seats. This measure alone will save billions of dollars, "yet no one knows about it" (Klein, 1994, p. 39). Remarkably it seems that even if the facts were proclaimed more loudly, a large percentage of the American public probably would refuse to believe that Clinton and not Bush or Reagan was the agent for such positive economic reform.

Another significant "revised fact" concerns the single biggest concern to millions of Americans—their income taxes. The facts of Clinton's 1993 "highest tax increase in history" were that 1.4 million of the wealthiest Americans had their taxes raised, while 15 million Americans had their taxes lowered (Kinsley, 1994). The myth that the middle class has suffered huge tax increases is indeed a myth, but it is a widely enough perceived myth that so far Clinton has been powerless to lessen its spread and its power. Michael Kinsley (1994) views the widespread misconception as the product of the realities of wealth and influence. "The 1.4 million whose taxes went up are a lot more influential than the 15 million whose taxes went down. The 'Clinton tax increase' hit people with family incomes over $185,000. This group included people like Jay Leno, David Letterman, and Rush Limbaugh" (p. 21). While Kinsley would no doubt admit that that one reason alone is insufficient to create all of the many misconceptions that clouded the Clinton presidency, it is difficult to argue with the belief that the 15 million families whose incomes were direct beneficiaries of the Clinton program were and are among the least heard and therefore least influential persons in our society.

Another reason that has been considered among those accounting for Clinton's early lack of popularity and for the huge Republican gain in the 1994 elections is that Clinton had failed to cut the size of government as he promised. Again, myth has won out over reality. "So far more than 70,000 federal jobs have been eliminated. By 1997, the federal work force will be smaller than at any time since Johnson. Yet nearly 78 percent of voters in a 1994 *Washington Post* Poll thought Clinton had made 'little or no progress' in this area" (Alter, 1994a, p. 49).

Perhaps Clinton's greatest success to date has been in dealing with deficit reduction. His presence in the White House alone has meant that the words "deficit reduction" can be credibly uttered for the first time since 1980, at the very least. Although his critics might think that the deficit should have been cut more dramatically, "Clinton has cut it more deeply than any of his hypocritical GOP predecessors; the deficit will go down three years in a row for the first time since the 1950s" (Alter, 1994a, p. 49). Fred I. Greenstein (1994) describes such an achievement as a "nonincremental policy change" and as one that was "exceedingly difficult to bring to pass in the United States" (p. 590).

"Whatever else he did and whatever you may think of his proposals, Clinton in his 1993 State of the Union address took us from this dishonest dithering" about the deficit "into the reality zone" (Greenfield, 1993, p. 82).

Despite these achievements, Clinton received little credit. Clinton's approval rating at the traditional 100-day marker was lower than that of eight of his nine immediate predecessors, and in November of 1994, the period of the tremendous Republican gains in Congress, it hovered around 50 percent. There are many explanations of differing credibilities concerning such a low approval rating. One plausible explanation lies in the influence of popular media phenomena, like Limbaugh, who use the airwaves daily to verbally assault the President, downplaying his achievements while accentuating his failures and personal shortcomings. This explanation is particularly plausible given such a low approval rating after only 100 days in office, a time too short for much in the way of policy to be implemented. Most importantly, however, as the lack of support even 100 days into his term illustrates, is the "selective perception" based upon the "priming" argument.

Yet another likely reason lies in the inordinate, if indeed understandable, attention that the American public places upon its own short-term economic interests. Deficit reduction is not something the average American "feels," particularly in the short-term. John Kenneth Galbraith (1992) referred to the "culture of contentment" that prevails in America and nearly forecloses any long-term action if it might come at the expense of immediate gratification. Such short-term focus also explains why President Reagan can be seen as a budget-cutter, and a successful leader during and even after he had overseen a ballooning of the deficit. "Reagan's most remarkable strategic achievement was his ability to persuade the public that he was a staunch fiscal conservative at the same time that his adminis-tration went on one of the biggest domestic spending sprees in

U.S. history" (Plotkin & Scheuerman, 1994, p. 75).

Still another and perhaps the most plausible reason for Clinton's failing public perception comes from the near-militant hostility that his most ardent detractors exhibit toward him. Groups such as the National Rifle Association (NRA), the Christian Coalition and its largely overlapping "pro-life" crowd, and a motley mix of anti-gay, anti-minority, and anti-"feminist" persons make life for President Clinton much more difficult than for most, if not all, previous Presidents. "There have never been such hateful diatribes directed at the White House from religious leaders as in the past four years. Hillary Clinton has been especially vilified by groups on the Religious Right" (Wallis, 1996, p. 167). Jim Wallis presents numerous quotes from such Religious Right heroes as Pat Buchanon and William Bennett and leaders such as Pat Robertson and Ralph Reed that bring new levels of incivility to "religious discourse." Among the cited "targets" of the Religious Right, according to Wallis (1996), have and continue to be

> ...the poor, people on welfare, blacks, women, feminists, pro-choice advocates, liberals, liberal Jews, Democrats, the federal government, the media, gun-control advocates, legal-services lawyers, public-school teachers, other religions and even main-line church denominations, and homosexuals. (pp. 162-3)

Other authors, notably Theodore C. Sorensen (1996), echo this perception of the Religious Right and its "extreme" militance—militance which pursues Clinton with military-like zeal. Wallis quotes journalist Bill Moyers at length as Moyers describes his views of the Religious Right. Moyers' description so vividly describes this segment of the population's "dialogue" with Clinton that I shall quote it as well:

> They invoke separation of church and state to protect themselves against encroachment from others, but denounce it when it protects others from them.... They deplore the coercive

power of the state, except when they would use those very powers to force others to do "the right and moral thing" as they define it. They stand foursquare behind the First Amendment when they exercise their right to control others—sometimes with a vengeance and often with vitriol, as when Jerry Falwell circulated videos implicating the President of the United States in murder—but when they in turn are challenged or criticized, they whine and complain that they are being attacked as "people of faith"...they want it both ways. In the pursuit of power they take no prisoners and give no quarter. But confronted and contradicted, they take refuge in piety and self-pity. (Moyers, as quoted in Wallis, 1996, p. 172).

The release of the movie *The People vs. Larry Flynt*, in 1996, presented a rather cogent example of Falwell's hypocracy. Not long after he presented his videos lambasting the President while insisting that the "proof" of accuracy was a series of "interesting facts," he condemned the rather negative portrayal of himself in the movie. Falwell stands as perhaps the most vivid example of the blatant hypocracy that exists in extreme persons, that has, unfortunately, afflicted even the perceptions of mainstream religions interested in healing and the concepts of forgiveness and Christian love.

Clinton is still afflicted by widespread perceptions of flaws within his character. He is widely believed to have been an adulterer; he now admits to having avoided the draft; and perhaps his greatest style over substance error was the "waffling" on the pot-smoking issue. Instead of merely acknowledging its use at Oxford and regretting his "mistake," he told us that he had tried it but, in words that haunt his Presidency, "he didn't inhale." Widespread belief that the President lacks "character" encourages the phenomenon of selective perception. While many in the public might try to look at his record, many refuse to "inhale," particularly if they might breathe in knowledge of accomplishments they either do not believe have happened, or they are unwilling to attribute to Clinton.

"The Militance of the Anti-Clinton Forces"

President Clinton, it should be noted, maintained his own blocks of supporters as well. Groups such as labor unions (though less so after NAFTA), minorities, feminist organizations, and the poor all lined-up largely, if not warmly, on the side of Democrats generally and Clinton specifically, yet the "militance" of these groups pales in comparison with those on the other side. Further, the support of these groups is not completely unified for a myriad of reasons, good and bad, unlike the near unanimous and sometimes passionate anti-support of the anti-Clinton groups.

Clinton's approval ratings, therefore, must be understood in the context of this period in history in which a significant portion of the public stood united against him, no matter what he might accomplish. A large and vocal portion of the public stood squarely against him from day one of his presidency, and it is probably not much of an exaggeration to proclaim that absent Clinton curing cancer (and probably even then) these groups will continue to work feverishly to get Clinton out of power, and/or diminish his standing. "Within ten days of taking office, he had 32 percent disapproval. So much for a honeymoon" (Edwards, 1996, p. 239).

Beyond the large segments of the public that relish presidential failure, the "loyal opposition" is perhaps more outspoken and surely more brazen than ever against a sitting president. Senator Jesse Helms, the chairman of the Armed Services Committee, has publicly proclaimed President Clinton "unfit to act as commander-in-chief." Other favorites of the far Right, such as Oliver North, have also publicly proclaimed not only their disdain for Clinton, but his "unfitness" for the office. The irony that many see when persons such as Helms and North proclaim their "concern" about "unfitness" is apparently lost on much of the electorate.

If ever there was a period in American history in which a

group of legislators wanted to see the President fail it may have been that period from Clinton's inauguration in January of 1993 until early in 1996. The evidence lies partially in the zealousness with which Clinton's opponents have blocked his initiatives, and can perhaps best be seen in the campaign reform legislation that the administration supported. That legislation was backed nearly unanimously until Clinton stood poised to use it as a victory, at which time the Republican Senators stood uniformly against the bill which they had stood uniformly for in the months leading up to its consideration. In May of 1994, the Senate voted 95-4 to prevent lobbyists from giving meals, trips, and other gifts to legislators and staffers. In October of 1994, 41 Senators backed a filibuster that killed the same bill (Alter, 1994b, p. 41).

Whatever motives the Senators may have had for keeping free trips and gifts, it is less clear about the motives of others who joined the bandwagon against the bill. The only thing these people had in common was hatred of President Clinton.

> At first Newt Gingrich said that under the bill any lobbyists who didn't register could go to jail. That was flatly untrue. Then the Christian Coalition said that the bill was a threat to religious lobbying, conveniently overlooking the clause that exempted religious organizations. Pat Robertson and Rush Limbaugh paired up to generate thousands of letters decrying the bill as a "gag order" on free expression. (Alter, 1994b, p. 41)

Whether the motives were to keep the golf trips or to simply prevent a Presidential "victory," it was clear that the minority party through the use of the filibuster had again thwarted the will of the majority. The trouble for Clinton was that only interested political observers actually paid attention to the facts, while millions of Limbaugh listeners and Christian Coalition supporters received significantly altered "facts" that played very well into their carefully honed "selective perceptions."

Every President has his detractors from both within and outside of his party, but Clinton's enemies list not only includes traditional Republicans, it is filled with well-organized, well-funded foes. His support for certain "gun control issues," such as the banning of assault weapons, means that the NRA hates him. His support for abortion rights means the Christian Coalition and many other anti-abortion groups hate him. His efforts to abolish the ban on gays in the military mean that the homophobes hate him. These powerful groups are among those who oppose Clinton not only with every fiber of their being, but more importantly with every resource that they might command.

"If It Looks Like a Duck, and Quacks Like a Duck, It Actually May be a Snake"

In the children's story the "Gingerbread Man," the title character accepts a ride from a fox in order to cross a stream. Although the fox exudes kindness toward the gingerbread man, he still, in the end, consumes him. Another variation on the story involves a snake who is befriended by and then befriends another animal, only to later bite him. When the victim asks the snake why, the snake can only say that "it isn't personal, I'm a snake, that's what I do." One cannot help but imagine the parallel between these stories and the 1994 elected Republican controlled House and Senate acting "cooperatively" with the Democratic President. While each one "reached out" toward the other, the public must surely realize that ultimately it was the goal of each side to "consume" the opponent.

It can be argued that Clinton, particularly during the debate over NAFTA and campaign reform, actually did reach out and attempt to work in a bipartisan manner. Jones (1996) viewed such "cross-partisan bargaining" as a hopeful mode of national policymaking, one that might overcome the hostilities between the players. Unfortunately, whatever value there may have been, and however productive cooperation might have been, the near results of NAFTA, and the actual results of campaign reform, illustrate that the President's hand was indeed nearly bitten off. If President Clinton can unify *this* government, it would be an act of statesmanship unheard of in recent, and not too recent, American political history.

Unfortunately for Clinton, and as profoundly illustrated by the day after the 1994 election shift from Democrat to Republican by Alabama Senator Richard Shelby, the later party shift by Representative Ben Nighthorse Campbell, and the filibuster that killed campaign reform, Clinton's chance to work with true control of both houses of Congress was short and significantly less real than the majority numbers indicated. Unlike Presidents Reagan and Bush, Clinton could not get the unified support from his own party that would have made his majority more legitimate. It is, of course, arguable that the reasons layed in the strength of their agendas rather than in the free will of their respective party members; yet, whatever the reason, Clinton's majority was more myth than reality.

Again the myth is far different from the reality of the 1980s, in which Reagan overspent and/or undertaxed madly. It was the policies pursued by Reagan and Bush that deserve at least as much if not more blame for the ballooning debt than does a Democratic Congress. However, the results of the 1994 elections that repudiated the work done by both the House and the Senate tell us that the American public largely blames Congress more than the President for our mountainous debt.

According to Kevin Phillips (1994), the Republicans, who developed a 1980s strategy of "borrow and spend" that matched any past Democratic laxity, would have been hobbled by controlling both the executive and legislative branches. Facing waves of red ink in that situation, they would have been unable to point, as they happily did, at congressional Democratic spenders and say "they did it, folks; they're the ones." Ultimately, of course, for the twenty years out of twenty-four of divided government, neither side had the full responsibility for choosing between hungry consitituencies and a more sober fiscal policy (Phillips, 1994, p. 117). Such a lack of "responsibility" has been, at one time or another, a boon to both parties. Nowhere perhaps is this more easily seen than in the political football that has come to be known almost generically as "deficit reduction." During the period between Clinton's election and the November 1994 election, the deficit actually declined.

The schizophrenia of the voting public is illustrated by two works a decade apart. In 1983, Seymour M. Lipset and William Schneider cited a 1980 poll that found that 51 percent endorsed the view that "when a president and a congress are of opposite political parties, it gives balance to our government," as opposed to 36 percent who believe that "we need a president and congress to be of the same political party to enact laws efficiently and quickly" (Lipset & Schneider, 1983, p. 38). The belief that control by one party of both Congress and the Presidency leads to less responsibility was and is belied by the facts, but, as usual, perceptions and style have triumphed over substance.

Nothing is more true than the adage that "change is constant in politics." By 1994, Phillips believed that the public was readying itself for "responsible government" in the form of control of both congress and the presidency by one party. In assessing the years since America has had a deficit, Phillips (1994) pointed out that the annual federal budget deficit rose from $9 billion in 1970 to almost $300 billion in 1992. During the years of "separated powers" from 1969 to early 1977, the deficit jumped from near balance to $50 billion. Then during the next "separated powers" years, from 1981 to 1992, there was a surge from $74 billion to nearly four times that figure. Deficitry was clearly on a roll in both periods. "By contrast, during the Carter years from 1977 to early 1981, where Democrats controlled the entire government, the annual deficit increased by only one half, from $50 billion to $74 billion" (Phillips, 1994, p. 118). "No one seriously suggests that the separation of powers is good for economic management" (Phillips, 1994, p. 118). With the ability of hindsight, we now know that for whatever reasons, and there are many, the voters stayed with divided government in the fall of 1996 by convincingly reelecting a Democratic President and a Republican Congress.

Whether or not one's philosophical differences with a given party make total control by the other party extremely unpalatable, there is little room for argument that control by one party will indeed make "finger-pointing" extremely difficult to accept. Of whom much is given, much is expected; and in the politics of this country in recent history, the voters haven't given too much, and have probably expected even less.

"Upon Whom Much Blame Is Placed, Much Blame Will Settle"

In a situation in which the American public is faced with little actual knowledge of the abstract term "deficit," and is forced to rely on the words of others to convince them of not only the seriousness of the problem, but as to the cause of the problem as well, it is the party that is better at finger-pointing that will emerge victorious. Thus far, the Republicans have been much better at the "blame-game."

Imagine a scenario in which two young brothers have a fight and both emerge bloodied. The parents are left to assess the blame and mete out the punishment. Since the fight was outside of the parents' vision, they must rely on the evidence at the scene (usually minimal) and the words of the combatants (often highly suspect). In such a situation, who really is at fault is much less important than who is perceived to have been at fault. The perception is shaped by the combatants with little regard for truth and justice. If the American voter is the parent and the

Democrats and the Republicans are the combatants, then the American voter acting as parent seems to have bought the Republicans' pleas that "the Democrats started it." The elections of 1994 stand as evidence that the voters sent the Democrats to their room without their supper.

Perhaps the greatest irony of Clinton's Presidency, and Bush's too, has been the mood of the country which, apparently at least, often longs for a leader more like Reagan. Reagan's "toughness" and his willingness to cut spending, though belied by the reality, remain among the greatest myths of the twentieth century. The present fight in Congress over the proposed "balanced budget amendment" again brings us full circle back to Reagan's rhetorical skill in blaming Congress for unbalanced budgets based upon his own tax reduction and spending proposals. Such rhetorical skill "underscores the prevalence of political posturing rather than fiscal realism in the balanced budget campaign" (Kyvig, 1995, p. 113). As ably as Reagan blamed Congress for deficits, Congress, now led by Newt Gingrich (actual leader of the House and symbolic leader of both the House and the Senate), blames today's President and past Democratically controlled Congresses.

In reality and by any measure, Reagan's deficits surpassed those of any President since Franklin Roosevelt. For the first six years of the Reagan administration, deficits averaged $161 billion each year, compared to an annual average since 1950 of just $28 billion. Interest payments on the growing national debt increased rapidly both because the amount of borrowed money had more than doubled in seven short years and because interest rates were much higher than in earlier decades. By 1986, the cost of financing the public debt was nearly $120 billion compared to $60 billion in 1980 and $30 billion in 1970. It took 3.25 percent of the GNP to finance the national debt in 1986, compared to 2 percent in 1980 and 1.4 percent in 1970 (Peterson & Rom, 1988, p. 236). Despite these realities, the myth persists: Reagan as guardian of the public treasury, and Clinton as an old-line Democrat "tax and spender." Part of the Reagan legacy surely lies in the duration that these deficits will have on future policy initiatives. Colin Campbell (1996) refers to

...two conditions that have greatly circumscribed presidential leadership: the deficit, which has created ceaseless pressures to reduce spending without raising taxes, and the sour public mood reflected in the anxieties about the accessibility of the American dream as the United States loses its economic dominance in the world. (p. 81)

Long-held perceptions are extremely difficult to overcome, largely due to what Moti Nissani (1994) calls "conceptual conservatism." Conceptual conservatism is the "cognitive tendency of human beings to cling to existing, strongly-held beliefs even after these beliefs have suffered decisive refutations" (Nissani, 1994, p. 307). So follows the oft-held belief that President Reagan was a "budget-cutter," while actually quadrupling the national debt. Whether or not "political conservatism" has truly taken hold in the U.S., "conceptual conservatism" and "selective perception" flourish.

The Myth of Reagan, The Reality of Clinton (Teflon v. Velcro)

It is nothing short of remarkable that the "successes" of the Clinton presidency have gone largely unnoticed, while, in contrast, the "failures" of the Reagan presidency went largely unnoticed. According to Rockman (1988), the Reagan presidency was organized around two seemingly contradictory elements: the Reagan style and the Reagan agenda. The style mostly appeared as soft and comforting, while the agenda mostly appeared as clear and polarizing (p. 9). Jones (1996) described Reagan's policymaking style as emphasizing goals more than

101

specific programs, relying heavily upon staff, and capitalizing upon his public persona. If Reagan was the "teflon" president, Clinton must surely be the "velcro" president.

Reagan's supporters believed that Reagan's policies brought a new morning of prosperity to America. His critics looked at the same policies and saw a disaster waiting to happen. Neither side is, as usual, completely correct. Still, as President Clinton is left to deal with a huge debt left over largely from the Reagan years, it is difficult to persist in the view that Reagan meant prosperity for America.

> The fear of rising deficits and the fear of higher taxes to pay for them make people more willing than ever to believe that much government spending, particularly the kind that does not help them, is ludicrously inefficient, wasteful, and excessive. (Plotkin & Scheuerman, 1994, pp. 27-28)

> Reagan's deficit will be around for decades, keeping the rightwing in charge of political priorities. The deficit, more than any other ideological factor in the current situation, conveniently legitimates elite indifference to economic stagnation and social need. The deficit has become the great elite excuse for avoiding economic activism. (Plotkin & Scheuerman, 1994, pp. 20-21)

Another noteworthy contradiction in the Reagan years, aside from the wild spending reality and the budget-minded myth, is the fact that Reagan enjoyed wide support while pursuing goals not supported by the broad public that liked him personally: goals such as an unbalanced budget, the Strategic Defense Initiative, contra aid, and the shipping of arms to Iran. In contrast, Clinton has undertaken many issues in which large segments of the American public are in agreement; issues such as healthcare reform, tax increases on the wealthy, campaign reform, stricter gun laws, campaign finance reform, and lobbying reform all garner tremendous support, and yet despite this consensus, it is Clinton's inability to make us "like him," and the underlying concerns about his "character," that may ultimately seal his historical, if not his political fate, far more than any disagreement with his policies.

If any lesson is to be learned from this, it is a harsh one. If it is indeed more important to be "liked" than to do positive works, then it is indeed a sorry state to which our political system has come. Isaac Asimov noted "I'm afraid that Ronald Reagan has, in a sense, weakened and trivialized the presidency, that he has... made it more important for a president to be popular than to be effective" (Asimov, 1987). President Clinton's initial effectiveness had been undermined by his inability to be "popular," and however painful that may have been to him personally, it has been far more painful to those seeking "reform." The need for popularity is belied by the constant polling that "analyzes" both party's initiatives and usually gauges how loud any future support might be. Popularity is much more than a vanity issue in presidential politics, as support for the President by members of Congress is significantly related to how that support will translate for the individual congressperson politically.

"Better to be Principled and Simplistic"

"One of the reasons why the American people seem to forgive Reagan so much is that they recognize in him a man of principle, even a utopian. But his utopia is, whether he knows it or not, a cover-up for the realpolitik of the rich and corporations" (Harrington, 1984, p. 254). In 1984, Michael Harrington wrote prophetically about Reagan as responsible for discrediting the notion of a principled and programmatic politics. "I can easily imagine the adepts of a stale wisdom arguing that any attempt to think things through, to meet economic and social problems in a systematic fashion, is doomed. Ronald Reagan could, in short, make 'muddling through' popular again" (Harrington, 1984, p. 254). Aaron Wildavsky (1988) cited Reagan's disinterest in, and misstatement of, facts about many aspects of public policy, not as a lack of intelligence, but instead as "superb political strategy" (p. 290).

> By undertaking a very few major initiatives, with widespread consequences, he is seen as a positive leader. By reserving his imprimatur for only the matters he considers most vital, he makes an infrequent target. By disclaiming intimate factual knowledge of specifics, he reduces the expectation that the President is responsible for whatever is disliked. (Wildavsky, 1988, p. 304)

Today, as we reflect upon the "failures" of President Clinton and his healthcare reform particularly, within the context of the overwhelming Democratic defeats of November 1994, we see that in America many wanted and want less government, and less of an attempt to meet economic and social problems in a systematic fashion. Instead many long for the "muddling through" of President Reagan and the lack of vision that President Bush so ably represented. President Clinton's "reluctant" agreement to support the "end of welfare as we know it" also illustrates his apparent belief that adhering to principles is too politically dangerous to handle. Rockman (1996) refers to Clinton's "desire to be liked" and his "pliability" as both a strength and a weakness. Not unlike Reagan, Clinton is described as "an extraordinarily ebullient man with an overriding sense of optimism" (Rockman, 1996, p. 349). Unlike Reagan, he is also described as having "intellectual agility" (Rockman, 1996, p. 354) that seems to have allowed this very complex man to win for himself a second term in office.

"If at First You Don't Succeed, Stop Trying"

The contrasts personally and presidentially between Reagan and Clinton are striking. Many applaud a leader like Clinton who takes on difficult and even controversial tasks (healthcare reform, gun control legislation, gays in the military), but it appears most will only applaud those undertakings if they are successfully completed. The mass of the voting public applauds loudly when success is to their direct benefit, but criticizes even more loudly when policy initiatives fail. Unlike what our parents told us when we were young. in politics to try but fail is much worse than not to try at all.

President Clinton's remarkable political turn-around relied upon his knowledge of the evidence of the contrasts between the myths and the realities of recent presidencies. These contrasts seem to require that he worry less about the realities and address many of the myths that have gained widespread acceptance. Robert E. Denton, Jr. (1988) perhaps put it best: "the nation's mythic, heroic, and symbolic expectations of the office are no longer apropos to meet the challenges of the twenty-first century" (p. 94). Addressing the myths and avoiding the realities seems to be a sure method of success.

Addressing reality was the goal of President Carter's 1979 "crisis in confidence" speech, for which he heavily relied on his pollster's evidence that Americans were increasingly disillusioned with most big institutions, were becoming more conservative, and were growing weary of costly big government. When Carter reminded his listeners that "the strength we need will not come from the White House, but from every house in America," Reagan was all too ready to step in and tell us that he would restore our confidence for us. While many feel that Reagan's was a failed presidency in reality, it can hardly be disputed that it not only handled the myths—indeed, it mastered the myths. It is a danger that Clinton's Presidency, even a two-term Presidency, may go down as successful in reality, but perish in the larger myths that seem to matter most to the electorate.

Chapter Summary

To some extent it strains credulity to believe that the press is capable of varying its behavior from administration to administration or in shaping public opinion in such significant ways. It should be noted that Limbaugh and other influential (if fact-flawed) conservative forces were against Clinton prior to his election, and Clinton did win. It is impossible to determine however, how much of an impact these forces had upon a close election in which an incumbant ran an ineffective campaign, after a divisive and polarizing convention, against a young, vigorous, competent (if flawed), and relentless campaigner. This chapter suggests that the public wanted change at almost any cost, and but for militant opposition to Clinton and the beginnings of an effective "revisionist" period, Clinton's victory and Bush's loss would have been much more decisive.

If, in fact, the public is more immune to the press than this work gives them credit for being, or if the press on balance depicts fairly the achievements and failures of this or any administration, then only Clinton and his immediate staff were to blame for the public's unwillingness to accept their word and their inability to effectively set the record straight. Regardless of who was to blame, Clinton was faced with the necessity of revising accepted public opinion concerning his leadership and his accomplishments. It is both the bane of our existence and the promise of our adaptiveness that "accepted public opinion" can be so dynamic. Perhaps as we more fully understand the fragility of public opinion we might be less inclined to be swayed by those who view "facts" as beliefs and "beliefs" as facts.

Bert A. Rockman (1996) offers the observation that it is difficult to make conclusions about "this unusual presidency that seems endlessly to be in political trouble, despite an economy that has boomed without inflation during Clinton's incumbency and despite the incumbant's own centrist and deal-cutting tendencies" (p. 356). Even such respected scholars as Rockman and Harold W. Stanley, both cited in this work, have written pieces that, at this point at least, seem to have underestimated the political ability of President Clinton in an environment increasingly unfriendly to hands-on policymakers.

> Bill Clinton is a reasonable man, who continues to believe that government can be part of the solution and is not inherently a part of the problem. American politics, as it has evolved toward the end of the twentieth century, has made it difficult for a leader of his temperament and perspective to succeed. (Rockman, 1996, p. 358)

> Clinton may turn his fortunes around, giving life once again to the "Comeback Kid" label, but in the aftermath of the 1994 midterm, it seems more likely that Clinton will be the sixth one-term president of the last eight. (Stanley, 1996, p. 205)

The reelection of President Clinton in 1996 despite the formidable odds against him, as cited in this work and others, proves, perhaps better than prior years, that when it comes to Presidential politics, "it ain't over 'til it's over." Whether this election precedes a period of more civility and moderation as a natural reaction against the "extremism" that many believe the 1994 elections introduced remains to be seen. It does, in any event, bode well for a future in which politicians may come again someday to be seen as among the best and brightest our society has to offer, and as those who will be allowed to formulate positive change while riding out the ebb and flow of negative public opinion.

Chapter Six
"Addressing School and Societal Violence through Greater Collective Responsibility"

While it is generally easier to criticize present responses to social problems than to offer more positive solutions, it is nevertheless valuable to consider the potential impact upon our youth and the consequent long-term harm of our society's increasingly strong "individualism" rhetoric and practice. This chapter considers the merits of the enduring social debate that has become dominated by voices urging the "virtue" of greater "personal responsibility" as a means by which to lessen many of our society's woes.

Introduction

This chapter examines the now prevalent rhetoric of "individualism" and "personal responsibility" and the implications such rhetoric and its by-products such as the "dismantling of the welfare state" have upon our increasingly violent society. Understanding the implications of the debate might actually contribute toward a lessening of the ever-growing problem of societal violence generally, and school violence in particular. Such an undertaking requires the recognition that the decline of our public schools and our civilization as we know it are both probably farther off than many of our social critics might believe. Whatever we, societally, do or do not do about the increasing levels of violence in our schools, most of our schools will likely continue to provide the best services they can, and in providing such services schools will continue to be effective for a majority of their students. There is danger inherent in considering such vague subjects as "violence" within such differing and unique settings as individual schools.

The uniqueness of each school situation limits the usefulness of general and overarching theories, unless these theories can be adapted to fit the needs of given schools facing different levels of violence. Within these adaptations of theory lies the need to gain a better understanding of the wider social theories that drive social policy. This chapter attempts to promote a further consideration of a growing social theory that considers the "individual" above the "group."

> Man is not self-sufficing in social isolation,...and that between man and such social groups as the family, local group, and interest association there is an indispensable connection. We know no conception of individuality is adequate that does not take into consideration the myriad ties which normally bind the individual to others from birth to death. (Nisbet, 1990, p. 205)

How society might lessen the ever increasing violence that afflicts us all has been the subject of an enduring social policy debate. While the quantity, volume, and intensity of the debate continues to grow, a corresponding increase in the quality of the debate has been significantly less clear.

Among those with the loudest, most intense, and seemingly influential voices in American politics is Newt Gingrich. Just before the 1994 elections, about-to-be-Speaker Gingrich urged citizens to vote Republican as a way of putting an end to the rampant crime and decay in society that was then so profoundly symbolized, at least to Gingrich, by the Susan Smith case in South Carolina. Congressman Gingrich apparently believed, or at least his rhetoric implied that he believed, that decades of Democratic control in the House had overseen the decline of society. On the surface, it is impossible to argue that the United States in 1998 is less prone to violent crime, particularly among our youth, than it was in 1958, 1968, 1978, or even 1988. One need not go far beneath the surface, however, to discover that the reasons for increasing societal violence contain far greater complexities than congressional control by either major political party. This chapter offers a response to the rhetoric of Gingrich and other like-minded individuals in the larger form of suggestions for lessening school violence that is increasing an element of, and a natural reaction to, an increasingly violent society.

Speaker Gingrich, though well-meaning we must hope, seems to miss the point, as does his much celebrated "Contract with America." Much of the rhetoric of Gingrich and his fellow Republicans centers upon focusing Americans toward the achievement and advancement of greater "personal responsibility." On a visit to the presidential caucus state of Iowa on July 24, 1995, Gingrich sounded his familiar refrain: "Any program which defines Americans by group is wrong and is destructive to Americans. We want Americans to think of themselves as individuals, not with a group mentality" (Gingrich, 1995). Ideology and our society's ideological apparatus, which encourages debate on tiny questions in order to deflect attention from the big ones, and which perpetuates a myth of individual responsibility to the exclusion of attention on structural causes (see Kohn, 1986, pp. 180-181) plays rather handily into Gingrich's philosophy.

Our rugged societal persistence in clinging to the ideals of "individualism" is baffling to those seeking social change. Even many members of the underclass in America often seem less committed to ending a system of privilege than in becoming privileged themselves. "They rarely challenge the basic script, preferring to concentrate only on the casting" (Kohn, 1986, p. 180). The irony for the poor is that the words of Gingrich, and those who believe like him in emphasizing greater personal responsibility, tie in nicely with lessening public spending and support for largely social programs, including our public schools— programs that, if funded, might contribute greatly to the likelihood that many individuals might someday have their opportunity to become among the "privileged classes."

> The erosion or dismantling of public and communal provision of health, education, and welfare services associated with economic restructuring and the turn towards...flexible forms of capital accumulation is one of the contexts, if not for some *the* context, in which the idea, and the necessity, of individuals looking after themselves, making choices and thereby supposedly assuming more responsibility for their care and their fate has been increasingly advanced. (Smart, 1995, p. 93)

Consciously choosing not to focus upon our "collective good," by instead focusing upon our freedom to seek individual accumulations of wealth, may or may not be "evil," but to those without power, it may seem so. Jonathan Kozol's 1995 work, *Amazing Grace*, uses the words of a young man from the South Bronx to eloquently describe "evil."

> I believe that what the rich have done to the poor people in this city is something that a preacher could call evil. Somebody has power. Pretending that they don't so they don't need to use it to help people—that is my idea of evil. (Kozol, 1995, p. 23)

Nathan Glazer (1988) wrote: "It can be argued that Americans are more likely to expect to make it on their own, and are scornful of those who do not" (p. 189). Scorn for those with less coupled with an uncanny ability to pretend that we societally cannot help has prevented genuine progress in improving the social order and, perhaps, in lessening violence. Glazer (1988) considers our conscious decision-making to be a "preference" that Americans have historically shown for individualism. We tend to exercise this preference even if it comes at the cost of improving the larger social order.

While one should not diminish the importance of some amount of greater "personal responsibility" in improving our society generally, it is the denial on the part of the privileged of any ability to lessen the suffering of the poor and the consequent support of individualism that is of greater concern. Our society must, of course, make economic decisions, but to deny that these decisions are in fact decisions, and are instead couched as "economic necessities," is fraud on a rather grand scale.

Likewise, "blaming" either the Democrats or the Republicans individually for our increasingly violent society is quite obviously overly simplistic and fatally flawed. More worrisome is that the act itself of seeking to "blame" others for problems for which we all share certain responsibilities goes some distance toward creating the type of dangerous society that the "blamers" themselves claim to despise. The futility and the danger of the "blame game" lies in the inability to ever win. If Gingrich believes that blame deserves to be assessed politically, there is plenty to go around, and rather than blaming decades of Democratic leadership in the U.S. House of Representatives, it may be in fact as much or more the recent policies of Republican presidential administrations that should come into question.

Steven F. Messner and Richard Rosenfeld (1997) contend that criminal activity is stimulated by strong cultural pressures for monetary success combined with anomie, a normative order with weak restraints on the selection of the means to pursue success (p. 97). "Economic dominance diminishes the attractiveness of alternatives to the goal of monetary success and impedes the capacity of other institutions to perform their distinctive functions, including social control. High levels of crime thus reflect intrinsic elements of American culture and the corrosive impact of these elements on social structure" (Messner & Rosenfeld, 1997, p. 97).

Violence in Our Schools

Whether or not attention to the plight of our schools and the increasing levels of danger present therein will "save" our schools and our larger society, increasing our attention to the problems facing schools—of which violence is a significant one—will likely allow us to better our schools, and thereby better our society. Perhaps we cannot make a "great leap for mankind," given our present economic, political, and social structure, but with effort we can make valuable, if rather incremental steps.

> Violence and disruption in schools does differ from crime in the streets, not only because it disrupts the learning process and diverts resources intended for educational purposes to pay for crime control, but also because, through the socialization process which takes place in schools, it can have a lasting effect on youth which spreads outward from the school over time. (Ianni, 1978, p. 21)

Any success that a school can achieve in educating its students can only come after assurances that the learning environment is safe. Just as the sciences have their prerequisites, achieving a level of comfort that is conducive to learning is a prerequisite for learning. School safety is the greatest threat to that comfort.

> Beginning teachers must recognize that preventing violence is an integral part of their legitimate work; the more effective they are at empowering youngsters the less violence they will engender; the less effective they are the more violence they will cause. (Haberman, 1994, p. 131)

Melissa Caudle (1994) recommended "8 Ways to Safer Schools," in an article entitled "Why Can't Johnny Be Safe? Eliminating School Violence." These "Ways" included: crisis management, zero tolerance zones, family approach (involving parents in education), environmental structure, cooperation between the schools and juvenile authorities, curriculum concerns, community involvement, and giving students a say. While supportive of the value of all of these ways, my approach emphasizes the last two: "community involvement" and "giving students a say." These two "safer school" suggestions offer the most benefit at the least cost, and in these tight budgetary times when schools are consistently underfunded while being attacked for not "getting the job done," achieving the greatest benefit at the least cost has never been more important.

"Actually, Greed Is Not So Good"

Elliott Currie (1995) distinguishes between a "market economy" and a "market society." In making this distinction, he asserts that there is nothing wrong with our use of a market economy. All societies make some use of market mechanisms to allocate goods and services. Assessing what the market does well and what is best accomplished by other means is often an empirical question. But "market society," he contends, is a different animal altogether. Currie (1995) defines market society as "one in which the pursuit of private gain becomes the organizing principle for all areas of social life—not simply a mechanism that we may use to accomplish certain circumscribed economic ends" (p. 61).

In a market society all other principles of social organization become subordinated to the overarching one of private gain. Alternative sources of livelihood, social support, and cultural value—even personal identity—become increasingly weakened, so that individuals, families, and communities are more and more dependent on what we somewhat misleadingly call the "free market" to provide for their needs—not only material needs, but cultural, symbolic, and psychic ones as well (Currie, 1995, p. 61).

According to Currie (1995):

> ...market society promotes crime by increasing inequality and concentrated economic deprivation; by eroding the capacity of local communities for support, mutual provision, and effective socialization of the young; by isolating the family and subjecting it to stress; by withdrawing public services from those already stripped of economic security and communal support; and by magnifying a culture of Darwinian competition for status and resources and by urging a level of consumption that it cannot provide for everyone.

Despite public perceptions and the rhetoric of the "Right," the communal aspect of such "collective" entities as public schools, labor unions, and cooperatives actually support capitalism and economic freedom. In such associations the goals of production, distribution, and consumption can be joined to the personal sense of belonging to a larger social order. For in such an association the individual can find a sense of relatedness to the entire culture and thus become its eager partisan. The individual entrepreneur is actually less dangerous to the totalitarian than the labor union or cooperative. Economic freedom is dependent upon the associational realities of collectives like labor unions and cooperatives, not the imaginary motives of the individualist. But unfortunately, there are still large areas of the economy and large segments of public opinion that are inclined to treat such associations as these as manifestations of collectivism, all a piece of the authoritarian State. The mythology of individualism continues to reign in discussions of economic freedom. By too many partisans of management the labor union is regarded as a major obstacle to economic autonomy and as partial paralysis of capitalism (for a discussion of the value of collectivism, see Nisbet, 1990, p. 214-215; Engvall, 1995).

"Greed is good" was a popular attitude in the 1980s. The conservative policies of the 1980s and the rhetoric and policy of Presidents Ronald Reagan and George Bush promoted a market society that emphasized, by its values, personal gain over social responsibility. According to Currie (1995), among others, market society values tend to erode traditional American values, by deemphasizing community and social responsibility in favor of individualism. Loving thy neighbor may be extreme, but not recognizing one's neighbor and viewing him or her only in terms of lifestyle competition is surely a negative evolution from bygone days. As we societally seek to supercede social responsibility with personal responsibility, crime and violence becomes a more legitimate way to satisfy needs. Individualism has allowed material gain to become a "need" and has shifted family, community, and group identity into the less critical category of "wants."

Within this context of individualism, personal gain, financial enrichment, and market society generally, we have been hearing a constant din from many political leaders urging greater "personal responsibility." Unfortunately drowned out in this din is the fundamental underlying responsibility in a democracy—social and group responsibility. "Looking out for number one" and the personal responsibility that those on the Right have taken as their touchstone is a vastly different philosophy than social and group responsibility that might have us "looking out for our friends, families, neighbors, schools, and communities" as well as ourselves.

> The implied distinction between public and private and the associated reality of a shift or off-loading of responsibility from state to private individual is one of the themes currently preoccupying the modern polity. (Smart, 1995, p. 93)

While recognizing the value of a market economy, we need to discourage the increasing cultural acceptance of a market society. In doing so we need to recognize that changing the values of a society cannot happen overnight, and the outcome of a political election will likely have little to do with ultimate societal change. In contrast, societal change will likely require a "meeting of the minds" between Democrats and Republicans in order to impose a standard of practice upon mainstream America. Blaming one side or the other will have a tendency to entrench the increasing emphasis on a "market society," and further separate us into "winners" and "losers."

Schools as Receptacles of our Larger Culture

The fact that violence and disunity is on the increase in our schools is easily compared to the increase in violence and disunity on our streets.

> The historic idea of a unifying American identity is now in peril in many arenas—in our politics, our voluntary organizations, our churches, our language. And in no arena is the rejection of an overriding national identity more crucial than in our system of education. The schools and colleges of the republic train the citizens of the future. Our public schools in particular have been the great instrument of assimilation and the great means of forming an American identity. (Schlesinger, 1992, p. 17)

Arthur M. Schlesinger, Jr., goes on to describe what he sees as the "troubling" impact of ethnic and racial pressures on our public schools. That schools "reflect society" is hardly arguable, how we societally handle this reflection however tends to divide us. Carrying out the reflection analogy, if schools reflect society as a mirror reflects one's face, then the most effective way to alter how that mirror perceives our features is to address our own limitations, rather than by purchasing a less candid mirror. Unfortunately, many have attempted to alter the schools reflection of society without addressing the larger societal characteristics that shape what the school becomes. In other words, blaming the schools for violence is like blaming the mirror for the size of our nose and the increasing wrinkles on our face. We could put our money into a new mirror that might better accentuate the positives, or we might better spend our money on changes in our lifestyle that might alter the reflection the mirror sends

118

back. Blaming the public school "failure" to curb violence, and supporting less spending on social programs generally, is an attempt to change the reflections of society by looking into a more forgiving mirror, rather than addressing the painful lifestyle changes that might present a better reflection.

While promoting more "free-market" competition and greater tax and spending incentives for parents to "freely choose" to send their children to private school, persons such as our Speaker of the House want privileged parents and children to gain the advantage of seeing themselves in more forgiving mirrors. Such policy would have more value if these children only viewed themselves through the mirrors in their own houses and their own schools and their own neighborhoods. Unfortunately when they venture out into other neighborhoods and their reflections are cast out into foreign mirrors, their appearances may be less than what they had expected.

> The bonds of national cohesion are sufficiently fragile already. Public education should aim to strengthen these bonds, not to weaken them. If separatist tendencies go on unchecked, the result can only be the fragmentation, resegregation, and tribalization of American life. (Schlesinger, 1992, p. 18)

The Future Is in the Schools

Both literally and figuratively, "our future is in our schools." Not only are our children physically present within the schools, but how our schools deal with these children shapes the future for all of us. If our best hope for tomorrow lies in our youth, as it surely must, then perhaps the best method of instilling "values" and lessening the rampant problems of crime lie in our schools. We can consider the role of schools less, and preach "personal responsibility," or we can increase our attention to the public schools and preach greater "collective responsibility."

Bobby Kipper (1996) urges greater collaboration between

law enforcement officials and the larger community in order to lessen school violence. To do so requires, in Kipper's words, "the understanding that school crime and violence are community issues—not just school problems" (p. 26). According to Kipper, law enforcement officials continue to be frustrated by the denial of crime-related issues on school campuses. This issue heightens the need for stronger police/school partnerships and the need for greater education concerning services that can be provided by law enforcement and schools working in tandem. Law enforcement agencies can not only assist with dealing "after-the-fact" with crisis management, but can and should assist schools in crisis planning, prevention, safety audits, and in-service programs for faculty, staff, and students.

Any increase in social services, including greater officer interaction with schools, necessarily will increase our dollar costs. How we handle our wallets is at the crux of politics, and, therefore, at the heart of funding for public schooling, prevention programs, and other "social" programs. If there were no government and no governmental responsibility, then personal responsibility would be the only driving force behind our spending concerns. In the real world, however, it is not only how we spend our money that concerns us, but how others might treat us as human beings. Teaching students traditional values about respect, and treating others as they would like to be treated, is likely to become even less effective in a society increasingly bent on viewing personal responsibility as its foundation.

Violence within our schools has become an increasing concern for administrators, parents, teachers, and students. According to the American Psychological Association's Commission on Violence and Youth (1993), teenagers are 2.5 times more likely to suffer violence than persons over age 20 and much of that violence occurs near schools. United States Education Department Secretary Richard Riley recently acknowledged that about three million thefts and violent crimes occur in or near schools each year (Riley, 1994; Haberman, 1994). "An explosion of media accounts indicates that violent behavior, resulting in injury or death, has become a pervasive feature in American schools" (O'Donoghue, 1995, p. 102).

Not everyone believes that crime in the schools has reached epidemic proportions. Gary K. Claybaugh (1994) believes that the studies that suggest disturbing trends toward violence are often small-scale, ill-conceived, or ideologically biased, and as such he cites "the media's school violence fad" as a "probably greed-motivated exploitation of a comparatively few sensational incidents" (p. 63). R. Craig Sautter (1995) similarly cites Federal Bureau of Investigation statistics to conclude that "the public perception that more young people than ever are in trouble with the law is incorrect" (p. K3). Sautter (1995) does conclude, however, that "the kinds of crime that young people commit are more serious today than in the past, and youthful criminals are becoming younger and younger" (p. K4). Gary D. Gottfredson and Denise C. Gottfredson (1985) perhaps give the best description of the state of school violence:

> ...the evidence suggests not that we have an acute crisis in school discipline or an increasing rebellion against order; it suggests rather that we have some chronic disciplinary problems in many schools. (p. 183)

Whatever the appropriate number of violent acts, and whether or not the perceptions of increasing violence in the schools as heightened by media attention are appropriate, the perceptions do persist and, as in society at large, fear of violence garners increasing attention politically and socially. Facing such a reality, alternate views which condemn the schools for "allowing" such violence, or excuse the schools as simple reflections of the larger society, contribute little toward a lessening of the problem (both real and perceived). Similarly, grandiose pronouncements foreseeing the decline of our civilization as we know it if we continue our present course are ineffective hyperbole which tend to gloss over the eyes of the reader and close the ears of the listener.

Throughout the 1980s it was customary to regard school violence as a phenomenon confined mainly to the nation's troubled inner-city schools (Baskin & Thomas, 1986; Evans & Evans, 1985). Joseph O'Donoghue (1995) pointed out that such an interpretation of school violence as basically an inner-city phenomenon has been challenged in the 1990s (p. 101).

Consistent with this belief, the tendency whenever violence was reported in suburban or rural schools was to interpret the attacks as atypical events that were not part of a pattern of violence (Feder, 1985; Feschbach & Feschbach, 1982). Perhaps such interpretations have been behind the historical reluctance of schools to develop violence prevention interventions that are part of the social structure or normal functioning of the school. "More often, solutions to the problem have centered on social structures external to the school" (Astor, 1995, p. 106). Increasingly, such convenient thinking is being reshaped.

The Value of "Democratic Participation"

Carl D. Glickman (1993) talks grandly of "renewal of the schools." "For a true awakening of our schools, we must return to their central goal: democratic participation" (Glickman, 1993, p. 149). "Democratic participation" goes beyond abstract concepts such as "reform" and "renewal" and touches upon real-world results such as lessening conflict. Only in an environment in which democratic participation is valued and fostered will violence decrease. In other words, the best way in which to "get tough on crime" and lessen violence within the schools is to involve the community (everyone, even the potential violators, whoever they might be) in discussing and implementing appropriate responses to dysfunction.

By instilling in all the "value" of their involvement, there will be a necessary correlative decrease in the number of "devalued" persons (real and perceived) who tend to see little value in the personal integrity and property of others. Participation in decision making can improve the quality of decisions and promote cooperation if the right strategy is linked to the right situation. Linking the right situation with the right strategy necessarily requires that the decision of how much subordinate involvement is appropriate is best made using a contingency model (Hoy & Tarter, 1993). Regardless of how much involvement is deemed appropriate, even a minimal level of involvement is almost certain to improve the status (real and perceived) of those who were previously denied any involvement.

Jeanne Jourdan (1994) wrote of a program in South Bend, Indiana, in which community involvement in the lives of children can lead to a lessening of the violence. This program has been labeled "This is My Neighborhood—No Shooting Allowed." The objectives of the program are to give children the chance to alter the attitudes of their friends and neighbors by: (1) Increasing community awareness and emphasizing disapproval of the use of weapons as a solution to problems; (2) Increasing neighborhood pride and creating safe areas for children; (3) Introducing children to the criminal justice system as an institution that protects children from violence and promotes equitable solutions to problems; and (4) Uniting children to work toward viewing guns as instruments of tragedy instead of symbols of glamour (Jourdan, 1994, p. 21).

Violence and the means by which it is perpetrated have become endemic in the new subculture of the impoverished inner city—key elements in what has come to be known as the American underclass. The social, economic, and structural conditions that have created the urban underclass are by now well known. The national poverty rate has been increasing since about 1980, and so the number of poor has increased, especially in the central cities. The gap between affluence and poverty has also widened.

Conventional routes of upward mobility have been narrowed; the life chances of the children of the poor have grown progressively dimmer. With no legitimate prospects for the future, life quickly becomes a quest for immediate gratification. Weighing the consequences of present behavior against their future implications becomes a meaningless exercise.

Given a larger culture that increasingly defines personal worth in terms of one's ability to consume, and a social and economic situation where one's ability to consume often depends on being able to take what one wants, any sense of personal merit (or self-esteem) rather quickly comes to imply being stronger, meaner, and better-armed than the next person. Blood flows where life has no purpose (Wright & Sheley, 1995, p. 188-89). To stop the flow of blood, our children have to be convinced that their lives have purpose and hope.

In the late 1980s, economists suggested that crime is prevalent because the risks of punishment are low and the profits are higher than the wages of traditional careers. Scholars studying urban America are debating whether or not the structural transformations of the 1970s and 1980s have created a qualitively as well as a quantitavely new dynamic of poverty different from the one faced by new immigrants at the turn of the century or prior to World War II. As our cities have shifted from manufacturing to service economies, high school graduates can no longer find stable, unionized jobs that provide health and retirement benefits and pay a family wage (Bourgois, 1995, p. 51).

The central cities, and consequently their schools, have become remarkably unsafe because of decades of indifference to their social and economic problems. Such indifference has bred an entire class of people with no stake in their own futures. Isolation, hopelessness, and fatalism, coupled with the steady deterioration of stabilizing social institutions and the police's inability to maintain security, breed an environment where success implies predation and survival depends on one's ability to defend against it. Widespread joblessness and few opportunities for upward mobility are the heart of the problem. Stricter gun control laws, more aggressive enforcement of existing laws, a crackdown on drug traffic, police task forces directed at juvenile gangs, metal detectors at the doors of schools, periodic locker searches, and shake-downs of students are inconsequential compared to the true need: the economic, social, and moral resurrection of the inner city (Wright & Sheley, 1995, pp. 192-93).

The Role of Teachers

According to Martin Haberman (1994), teachers' roles in all of this are to "create a school experience in which students succeed and relate to one another in ways not determined by the threat of force and coercion" (p. 132). Haberman refers to this as "gentle teaching." Recognition that school experiences can only get better classroom by classroom and teacher by teacher will also contribute to successful implementation of a plan to lessen school violence.

Involving Parents and Students in Creating Rules of Behavior

As a means of providing help to schools seeking answers to violence problems, this section offers practical advice on how administrators, teachers, and parents might contribute to a lessening of violence within their schools by suggesting more than generic pleas for "reasonableness" and "fairness," however well-reasoned those pleas may be. The best manner in which to achieve "reasonableness" and "fairness" is to include the "judges" of those attributes in the decision-making process. In other words, including parents and students in the process of promulgating a "rule" book for the schools will increase the likelihood that such a rule book will be understood, respected, and therefore adhered to. Once such a policy book is in place, yearly review is necessary to continue to ensure the on-going "participatory decision-making" of students and parents. Gottfredson and Gottfredson (1985) put it thusly: "the more clear, explicit, and firm the running of the school, the less the disorder—in terms of both teacher and student victimizations—that the school experiences" (p. 173). Similarly, when students report that rule enforcement is firm and clear, or that the rules were fair and clear, their schools experience less disruption (Gottfredson & Gottfredson, 1985).

Such parental and student involvement is in direct contrast to what I will call "standard fairness and reasonableness handbooks" that most schools presently offer. These handbooks are usually unread and unconsidered, and therefore the guidelines for behavior that they propose are not usually debated until after a violation has occurred or has potentially occurred. By that time, it may be too late to gain consensus upon the legitimacy of the rule violated and consensus as to the punishment meted out.

Many of these handbooks consider the balancing test that courts must engage in to properly solve disputes, and/or they offer generic advice based on the legal maxims of "reasonableness" and "fairness." There is value in knowledge and awareness of court decisions in which a given court "has been forced to balance the students' constitutional protections from arbitrary and excessive discipline against the need for school officials to maintain order and discipline in the school setting" (Horner, 1993, p. 37). Still, what may be more helpful and more practically useful are suggestions for the real life situations that teachers, students, and administrators might routinely find themselves in. Knowledge that "for the most part, courts have been tolerant of school officials who give advance notice of prohibited behavior and administer punishment in a reasonable manner consistent with the due process rights enjoyed by the student" (Horner,

1993, p. 37) may comfort administrators, but such knowledge does little to alleviate stressful and potentially violent situations.

The best way for school administrators to steer clear of the courts, and the expense, bad publicity, and the consumption of time and effort that defending a school decision in court requires, is to prevent problems from occurring and when problems do occur to resolve them as quickly and painlessly as possible. To most effectively do so requires parental, community, and student involvement. Carl D. Glickman (1993) believes that "in schools where there is a push to include, listen to, and invite people to participate, there will be less apathy and fewer complaints" (pp. 144-45).

> Truly democratic schools, by definition, will have more people contributing and less dysfunctional behavior because the responsibility for turning the behavior around rests with the entire school community rather than with one person in authority. (Glickman, 1993, p. 145)

Goran Ahrne (1994) addressed the "continual interplay between organizations and institutions." The interplay between organizations such as schools with institutions such as the law provide ample opportunity for confusion to develop between the appropriate role of each. Laws are prohibiting; they state what you must not do. Unlike organizational rules, laws do not generally tell you what you should do (Ahrne, 1994, p. 84). Often school "rules" which should describe appropriate conduct attempt to become laws prohibiting certain conduct. More than a matter of semantics, the distinction between laws and rules can be helpful to school administrators when rules are broken. The breaking of "rules" leads to punishment, based on the circumstances, properly meted out by the administration. The breaking of laws leads or should lead to prosecution by an outside authority: the courts. Becoming involved in juvenile justice is not appropriate for schools; whereas becoming involved in orderly juvenile discipline by adherence to rules is appropriate for schools.

The Dilemma of Punishment and "Problem Transference"

"Discussions of punishment in schools usually contain a mishmash of metaphorical and legalistic concepts with little attention paid to using consistent, much less moral, criteria" (Rozycki, 1994, p. 87). When punishment is considered, there are differing and critical issues to consider. Beyond the need for administrators to act in accordance with the law lies the need for administrators to act in the best interests of their school, and the need to have at least a passing awareness of the implications upon the larger society of actions taken within the schools. Among those implications is "problem transference," or the fact that suspensions and particularly expulsions from school may merely transfer the "problem" to another forum, usually society at large. In recognition of the need for society to attempt to prevent such ineffective transfers, school administrators must do all within their power to prevent problems from occurring, and when problems do occur, they must do everything reasonably possible to prevent their future occurrence, either within the schools or on the streets.

Our national failure to reduce aggression in America's schools is in large part a failure of perspective. According to Arnold P. Goldstein, et al. (1984), "viable controls, alternative models, and prevention techniques do exist, but they have been utilized in a piecemeal, often unsystematic, and, especially, unidimensional manner" (p. viii). When violence occurs, corrective steps must not only focus upon the teachers, students, and school involved, but also upon the community from which the violence arose. Goldstein, et al., (1984) advocate a systems approach in which "optimal interventions should occur concurrently at the student, teacher, school, and community levels" (p. ix).

While recognizing that "turning violent and disruptive kids out onto the street will not help them," the late Albert Shanker (1994) was among those who were concerned about the tendency in our society to forget the victims of violence and disruption and overly concern ourselves with the violent and disruptive actors.

> Why do we place so much value on youngsters who come to class with knives or guns and so little on their classmates who want to learn—or would give it a try if their classes were not disrupted by violence or fears of violence? (Shanker, 1994, p. 7)

Prevention of problems requires attention to foreseeable problems and a mechanism for dealing with problems once they occur that not only realistically addresses the specific problematic occurrance, but also confines the problem and diminishes the chances of problem growth. In order to effectively limit problems from spreading and to effectively deal with problems themselves schools need to separate the punishment for the behavior, from the person whose behavior needs punishment. Whatever a child lacks that causes that child to act out against others must be dealt with in addition to an effective termination of the problem behavior. Unfortunately, school discipline is often viewed as termination of a specific problem confronting the administration, and not as an effective part of the entire operation of the school environment.

"Can't We All Just Get Along?"

Questions over how schools can control student behavior will continue to provide sources of litigation. This litigation will range from complaints over locker searches to complaints over the due process allowed expelled students. Recognition that our litigious society will continue to expand the parameters of acceptable court cases is an important beginning point for any school administrator who is concerned not only with attempts to eliminate litigation but also with lessening the complexity of disputes when they occur. Many disputes arise and are exacerbated by a simple inability of one party to "understand" the other. Attempts to make one "understand" after a dispute arises are usually less successful than proactive attempts to insure "understanding" of acceptable boundaries of conduct prior to any disputes. Providing such a proactive understanding is easier said than done. Nevertheless by following simple guidelines focusing upon communication and information, administrators have the ability to significantly lessen the likelihood of disputes.

Steps toward Minimizing Violence

Most of today's public school systems have formal policies and rules specifically covering student discipline. These rules, often referred to generically as "student codes of conduct," specify the nature and severity of the student offense and include alternatives of punishment available for each (Vacca, 1993, p. 29). The need to avoid unnecessary and complicating vagueness is paramount; however, such avoidance must parallel the understanding that a guide covering all situations that might occur is impractical. Critical to lessening the severity of disputes over "behavior control" is that administrators should err on the side of due process. In other words, even in "simple" cases where the behavior is aggregious and the suspension is short-term, a student is entitled to the rudiments of due process. These rudiments should include: a written notice of the charges against the student, an opportunity for the student to deny the charges, a statement of evidence that school authorities actually possess, and an opportunity for the student to present his or her version of the incident (O'Reilly & Green, 1992). The sooner such a due process procedure takes place after the incident the better.

However time-consuming and annoying, administrators should provide written forms which they can send out to parents and to the student to inform them of *any* disciplinary action that was taken, however seemingly innocuous. Such complete documentation of all incidents that lead to discipline will prove invaluable in avoiding misunderstandings about the severity of punishment at later dates. (In these days of computer literacy, maintenance of forms in which names and pertinent facts can be inserted should be accomplished with little burden).

Another important consideration is enforceability. "Rules that are admired are most easily accepted, and most easily enforced" (O'Reilly & Green, 1992, p. ix). In order to promulgate rules that might be admired, the rules must first be understood and the rationale for their implementation must be advanced. One method in which understanding might be increased would be to involve the parents in the creation of rules. Not only would schools gain from the input of "outsiders," but it makes disagreement with enforced rules more difficult if it is felt that parents as well as school "insiders" were a part of the creation. Like most issues involving parental involvement in the public schools, using parents in order to help achieve written guidelines would not be free of all controversy.

In enforcement of any disciplinary code, the severity of punishment, ranging from expulsion from school to a visit to the principal's office, must be considered. Generally, the more serious the punishment, the more formalized and extensive the requirements of procedural due process (Vacca, 1993). Basic fairness is the rationale of contemporary procedural due process. Fairness should undergird every decision made by a governmental entity, particularly the public schools (Vacca, 1993).

Chapter Summary

The differences between many of the recommendations set forth by Richard S. Vacca (1993) and Melissa Caudle (1994), among others, are more in style than in substance. Some commentators, Vacca (1993) among them, set forth formal rules; Caudle (1994) in contrast, sets forth a tone of "common sense." Both sets of recommendations are useful, and are especially useful when they are considered together. By finding common ground in numerous sets of suggestions, and most importantly, by involving parents and other citizens in forming the groundwork for "codes of conduct," the rules set forth in the codes that are ultimately implemented will better prepare schools for situations that administrators had hoped would never occur by ensuring greater enforceability and greater acceptability.

Many of the terms of contemporary debate about juvenile violence—drugs, gangs, even guns themselves—are secondary problems. They provide a method of restating the problem but cannot suggest a solution. Guns, drugs, gangs, crime, and violence express a pervasive alienation of inner-city youth from the conventions of larger society. We—the larger society—can try to impose our will, pass new regulatory legislation, and promote harsher punishments for those who defy our rules. But until we rectify the conditions that breed hostility, estrangement, futility, and hopelessness, whatever else we do will come to little or nothing (Wright & Sheley, 1995, p. 192).

Likewise, until we "humanize" the environment surrounding the schools, we will have difficulty humanizing the environment within the schools. Few could suggest to teachers in violent schools that we simply eliminate metal detectors or guards in order to humanize their environment. Still,

...the urban schools that feel safe to those who spend their time there don't have metal detectors or armed security guards, and their principals don't carry baseball bats. What these schools have is a strong sense of community and collective responsibility. Such schools are seen by students as sacred territory, too special to be spoiled by crime and violence, and too important to risk one's being excluded. (Noguera, 1995, p. 207)

So, while we probably should not unilaterally "disarm" our school administrators, we must recognize that many safety assurances are concessions to the defeat of a human and caring school environment. Such concessions should not be granted lightly, and we should do all that we can to lessen the need for making such concessions necessary. Foremost among that which we can do is to recognize and advocate the merits of collective responsibility.

It's quite simple, really, in theory if not in practice. If I were to lose my wallet or if I were to be injured in an accident, it is my hope that the one finding my belongings or caring to my needs be a believer in his or her collective responsibility within our society. For it is in his or her collective benefit to give assistance when assistance is needed in the hope that such giving might be reciprocated if he or she is in need. Such giving of one's self is quite contrary to the virtues of personal responsibility, in which the finder of my wallet might condemn my absent-mindedness or the viewer of my accident might berate my carelessness long before they might extend their hand to help.

It is a matter more important and transcendent than politics that should and will determine how our nation's school children are influenced. It is largely through our example and our efforts to show our youth that we actually care about their welfare and care about their education. Anything less is merely a band-aid on a gun-shot wound: in some small way helpful, but largely missing the source of the pain, and completely missing the appropriate and lasting treatment.

Emphasizing the virtues of greater personal responsibility

probably can't hurt our troubled and violence-plagued schools, but emphasizing the virtues of greater collective responsibility is where our best hopes lie in truly bettering our nation's young people and thereby our nation's future. As we slowly begin to recognize the merits of preventative medicine, might we also begin to recognize the benefits of preventative maintenance on our children. Dollars spent on education now will likely be dollars saved in the future. We should not allow for the diminishment and reduction of so many largely effective social programs in however worthy an effort to save money in the present. Not because standing in the way of these cuts is the right thing to do politically, but because it is the right thing to do, period.

Chapter Seven

"The Price of Today's Contentment May Be Tomorrow's Increased Militance" or "The Virtue of Militance"

Introduction

This chapter consists of three separate and distinct, yet interrelated parts. Part 1 centers on the need for teachers to overcome what John Kenneth Galbraith so eloquently described as "the culture of contentment" that retards significant alteration of the status quo. Part 2 focuses upon the as yet unsolvable conflict between teacher autonomy and increased "professionalism" and public control over the schools. Part 3 concludes that what might be called the "macro-reform" debate, a debate which fails to account for the variances in circumstances across lines both visible and invisible, ought to be shelved, in favor of more attainable "micro-reforms" that center upon given circumstances in given definable and improvable settings and curricular areas.

> Those of us who have everything we need and, in general, make all the decisions about our society simply do not know those who are living in poverty, alienation, and despair. The families who find it difficult to get good jobs, decent homes, safe neighborhoods, and good medical care and education do

not know or trust their privileged neighbors, the court system, or the police to care about their plight. (Carter, 1996, p. 123)

The decisions we make concerning public education in this country could mean the difference between reestablishing the United States as the land of opportunity and becoming even more decisively a land of haves and have-nots. (Greider, 1992, p. 73)

The Need for Teachers To Address "the Culture of Contentment"

Galbraith's *The Culture of Contentment* set forth two general expressions of the "contented majority" that drive public policy. First is the affirmation that those in the "contented majority" are receiving their just desserts. "What the individual member aspires to have and enjoy is the product of his or her personal virtue, intelligence, and effort" (Galbraith, 1992, p. 18). The second important characteristic of the contented majority is its attitude towards time. "In the briefest word, short-run public inaction, even if held to be alarming as to consequence, is always preferred to protective long-run action" (Galbraith, 1992, p. 20).

The ramifications of these two expressions for education in general, and teachers and teachers organizations in particular, are quite significant. Two important implications spring immediately to mind: first, if large portions of the public regard teachers' present rewards are their own "just desserts," then there is little need to speak of increased pay; and second, if education is always determined to involve long-run benefits in return for immediate costs, then inaction will undoubtedly prevail in a contest with any sweeping "reform."

While recent elections indicate a pervasive belief that government in general has been viewed as a burden, there have been significant and costly exceptions from this broad condemnation. Indeed, the "burden" of government is a selective burden. Social expenditure favorable to the fortunate, financial rescue, military spending, and, of course, interest payments—these constitute in the aggregate by far the largest part of the federal budget and that which in recent times has shown by far the greatest increase.

> For the poor, the government can be central to their well-being, and for some even to survival. For the rich and the comfortable, it is a burden save when, as in the case of military expenditure, social security, and the rescue of failed financial institutions, it serves their particular interest. Then it ceases to be burdensome and becomes a social necessity, a social good, as certainly it is not when the government serves the poor. (Galbraith, 1996, p. 8)

Galbraith expresses his surprise at the "tranquility of the underclass" during this period of contentment, and puts forth the warning in the form of a question: "How long should we expect the 'tranquility of the underclass' to continue?" (1992, p. 41). The author asks that we consider Galbraith's question as a call to action in addressing the problems of the "underclass" with more than rhetoric. As for teachers, it is time to (figuratively) take to the streets in defense of your students for whom any real reform should be centered. If this is in conflict with "professional" status and "professional" aspirations, it is time to reexamine the decision made in which teaching was chosen over business, law, and medicine.

Teaching is truly a "different" profession that requires the attributes of different persons than lawyers, business executives, and doctors. It is time to increase the professional status of teaching by proving to society that among the professional differences is a tremendous interest in the common good that has often precluded serious interest in personal advancement. At a time when diversity is to be celebrated and students are encouraged to be themselves, why should the teaching profession feel such a need to be seen as one of the "standard" professions.

Greater success might be achieved if teachers' and their associations were to begin to argue that there is nothing "standard" about teaching, about students, or about the "profession."

> Teaching is a social practice whose importance is unquestioned, even if what makes it important remains the subject of continued debate. (Hansen, 1994, p. 266)

The extent to which education is genuinely valued in our society has often been called into question (Gardner, 1991). "The educational enterprise continues to be devalued by our society, our academic institutions, and even by us...part of the problem is caused by the simplistic way we think about it" (Weimer, 1993, p. 2).

> The lack of reward and recognition in part results from the simplistic, nonreflective, and uninformed ways many in our profession think about teaching. Approaching the teaching-learning enterprise in more intellectually robust ways puts you on the side of those of us committed to being part of the solution. (Weimer, 1993, p. 124)

Wide scale reform has, thus far, been so much talk and so little action. There is fairly wide-spread consensus that life in the great cities in general could be improved by public action—by better schools with better paid teachers, by counseling on drug addiction, by employment training, by public investment in housing, by adequately supported healthcare, recreational facilities, libraries, and police. "The question, contrary to the rhetoric, is not what can be done but what will be paid" (Galbraith, 1992, p. 181).

Four years after *The Culture of Contentment*, another Galbraith work still reflects his belief that "the prestige and the income of the teaching profession must reflect the high importance of education in the modern society. Education must both attract and celebrate the best" (Galbraith, 1996, p. 74). There has been much talk of educational reform; absent only has been the willingness to appropriate and spend public funds, especially on those schools in the central cities. "Without this willingness no significant educational improvement can be expected" (Galbraith, 1992, p. 181).

If the "culture of contentment" allows for little money to improve education, and if any real reform would require money, then perhaps the way to real reform is to chip away at the foundation of contentment. Altering such a strong foundation requires the expenditure of great energy on the part of teachers and their organizations in particular and organized labor in general in order to "shake-up" the complacent and contented majority presently unwilling to change what has been a personally favorable status-quo position.

Convincing teachers to assert themselves after years of being told to be quiet, take orders, and leave their ideas at the schoolhouse door, is going to be far more difficult than equipping principals with a new administrative style or showing parents how to run a meeting or read a budget.

> In the case of teachers, we're talking about altering a public image—indeed, a self-image—that is deeply rooted in social and educational tradition. Changing this image might be the single most difficult part of the needed cultural transformation. (Fiske, 1991, p. 254)

How Might We Accomplish Such a "Shake-Up?"

Whatever factor or factors that one considers the leading cause of our "decline," there is ample reason to believe that the schools, even if they share in the burden of responsibility, do not deserve all of the blame. Education is not the problem, it is the solution, it is and has been our society's "gateway to opportunity." Moreover, if education can give opportunity, a lack of education can take opportunity away (Goodwin, 1992, p. 146). "Getting the people behind the public schools" is not just the politics of annual budgets and bond issues. "Supporting the public schools is about living the values which the school stands for, whatever one's age" (Sizer, 1992, p. 27). This is the rhetoric that should be on the lips of teachers, administrators, and parents, not the social Darwinism made so popular by Ronald Reagan and now practiced without apology by Newt Gingrich and the Republican Congress.

Since we cannot change the educational environment within the homes in which our children live (a fact which seems to elude those citing the lack of concrete evidence linking spending to outcome), we might strive to make certain that, once those children enter the schoolhouse, they may have a decent, safe, and valuable experience—an experience that might instill in them and ultimately in their children the value that we as a nation place upon education. For the federal government to largely abdicate responsibility and argue that states and even localities know best, is to abandon any precept that we want all of our children to stand a fair, if perhaps not equal chance in this country regardless of where they were born. Amy Gutmann (1987) puts it most clearly: "a democratic state must take steps to avoid...inequalities that deprive children of educational attainment adequate to participate in the political process" (p. 134). The "culture of contentment" seems to indicate that we are content enough with our present state of inequality and our continually growing disparity among our citizens.

As Galbraith suggests, I think, such contentment masks an underlying reality and fails to address the impact upon all of us that "poor" social services have—particularly the impact that poor education has. Although a poorly educated student may not live in "my" neighborhood, or have daily contact with me, my taxes will be impacted adversely by that student's eventual lack of ability and productivity and ultimate failure to attain for him or herself the level that a good education might have made possible. While we cannot be certain if any of these poorly educated students might have gone on to cure cancer if they had been granted greater opportunity, we should also not be so certain that they would not. Beyond such abstract "hopes" lie many more concrete connections between poor educational opportunity and greater dependence upon other social systems.

Clearly, for example, many have long claimed that "poor" education plays an important role in increased crime (see *inter alia* Hirschi, 1972; West & Farrington, 1973). Other studies claim that poor educational opportunities or the failure of the educational system to meet the needs of constituents leads to increased dependency, and decreased productivity, but despite our knowledge of the connection, we seem all too able to ignore any connections that do not presently and directly impact us.

Amitai Etzioni (1993) wrote: "If the moral infrastructure of our communities is to be restored, schools will have to step in where the family, neighborhoods, and religious institutions have been failing" (p. 89). In sharp contrast to Etzioni's "communitarian" beliefs, policies which seek to lessen the importance of public schooling and which allow the federal government to approach a "hands-off" attitude toward public education go hand in hand with tax and social policies that seek division among the people.

It is the "culture of contentment" that does not allow room for reform that would center upon bettering the lives of those at the bottom and middle income class levels at the expense of those at the top. Healthcare reform and education reform tend to get sidetracked, as powerful interests like physicians and the American Medical Association, insurance companies, and parents residing in wealthy districts tend to lobby effectively against them. In contrast, "welfare reform," which seeks to spend less money (and soon) on those at the bottom of society, while saving money for those in the middle and at the top, tends to gain almost universal support, as recently made clear by President Bill Clinton's signing of the bill to "end welfare as we know it," despite the vocal protests of many influential "liberal" thinkers. While it may be (and surely is) politically expedient, it takes very little political courage to stand up against the poor, underprivileged, and usually underrepresented elements of our society.

Complacent "Professionalism" in a Cold, Cruel World

We have all been familiarized with the old connundrum concerning the "chicken and the egg." Talk of teacher "professionalization" brings forth the profundity of that old story. As Marc Tucker of the National Center on Education and the Economy put it: "You can't improve schools without good teachers, but you can't get good teachers unless you treat them as professionals" (Fiske, 1991, p. 259). Perhaps the quote should suggest that you can't get "better" teachers unless you treat them as professionals. In any event, the debate is aptly framed by the "chicken and egg" debate, but is perhaps best understood as a continuation of the "myth of Sisyphus." Just as Sisyphus could never attain his goal, any education reform proposal will also not be able to reach the crest of the hill without the willing involvement of everyone in the schools. Teachers (and their unions) will have to have a responsible role in designing and carrying out educational reform, instead of having reforms dumped on them (Rosow & Zager, 1989).

Such a realization and understanding of the "chicken and egg" phenomenon is necessary to properly evaluate the various school reform proposals and to understand why none of them has any great chance for success so long as they compete against one another substantively and rhetorically. This realization brings us to the dilemma in the public schools of public control versus professional autonomy. The dilemma is long-standing and well grounded. Since public democratic control of the public schools is historically, politically, legally, and socially established, there is a view that however valid increased "professionalization" might be, it cannot actually be implemented to any real degree.

"The central category of analysis in the sociology of the professions is autonomy, or the authority to assert control over work" (Seron & Ferris, 1995, p. 22). Increasing teacher "professionalization" by increasing teacher autonomy seems to be rather unrealistic in present day America. The intrinsic link between public education, community and national identity, and the future (children) assures us that, as in the past, schools will continue to be a political and legal battleground (Hunter, 1991). Such a battleground will likely continue to be seen as too important to be left to the "uncontrolled discretion" of teachers. In light of that and other realities, many writers, such as Roger Soder (1990) and Gary D. Fenstermacher (1990), have considered the possibility that teachers might be well-served by forgetting their aspirations toward professionalization in order to more realistically focus on teaching as a vocation or calling.

If we can recognize what hasn't worked, perhaps we might come closer to what might actually work. One method of addressing teachers' concerns might come through toning down the rhetoric about the status that teachers have been relegated to in our society. Instead of lengthy platitudes about "professionalism," and the complacency that such eloquence seems to foster, teachers might be better able to advance themselves as a profession generally by greater focus upon their union roots and a return to a more "militant, activist" posture.

Michael Goldfield (1987) concluded that "unions that are more aggressive and militant, or that are at least perceived as such, seem to have more success than those that are not" (p. 226). Essentially, teachers might consider improving their "status" by limiting their concern about their present "status" in favor of promoting the interests of their students first, in their rhetoric as well as in their actions. The hope would be for teachers to "depersonalize" their rhetoric. One method to "depersonalize" their rhetoric might be found in a transition to a more activist, traditional "blue collar" union model.

Who, than teachers, might better teach the masses that greater worker empowerment and more effective and better worker organizations remains "a major civilizing factor in modern economic life" (Galbraith, 1996, p. 66)? While we societally concentrate upon stable prices and lower taxes, we move further toward what Galbraith (1996) referred to as "private affluence and public squalor" (p. 97).

> The private living standard is the beneficiary of enthusiastic, often relentless advocacy; that is the function of all salesmanship, all advertising, all product and service promotion. By contrast, the public living standard—schools, parks, libraries, law enforcement, public transport, much else—has no such support. The consequence, one that is wholly familiar, is expensive television and meager schools, clean houses and dirty streets... (p. 97)

Since the public has been largely unmoved by the pleas made by teachers for more money and/or greater benefits, and there is no reason to believe a change is in the offing, it may be time to change the entire debate—from a debate on greater professionalization that would thereby "improve education" towards a debate on the schools themselves in the hope that school improvement, and greater public concern and support for the students, might be accompanied by an increase in the status and treatment of teachers by the taxpayers.

Teachers and their organizations, rightly or wrongly, carry a public perception of weakness and indecisiveness that has not served them particularly well. One way that the "strength" of teachers might be increased would be a merger of the National Education Association (NEA) and the American Federation of Teachers (ATF) into a more powerful, more decisive unit. Even absent a merger, however, the strength of the two organizations could be increased by more vocal opposition to "reform" proposals that quite clearly lay the blame for any deficiencies within society at the doorstep of the public schools, rather than at the doorstep of the larger society of which the schools are merely a part.

The word "professionalism" has been used for years in an attempt to explain the status and proper role of teachers. The word "profession" in describing teaching has "in a strange and perverted way connected professionalism with long-suffering duty and and compliant, unquestioning response to authority" (Kerchner, 1992).

In this era of "reform," a more activist stance by teachers might allow for a more productive debate on "reform" by shifting the focus away from national and state proposals toward the needs of local districts. The benefits to children could be substantial, as more attention might be necessarily placed upon districts in which the educational opportunities afforded children are glaringly unequal in comparison to other districts.

In an address to the NEA's national conference in 1992, Charles Kerchner sought to dispel the "myth that unions are inflexible and unchangeable." In dispelling that myth, Kerchner sought to focus the teachers' unions toward a new orientation, the idea that unions can be organized around groups of employed "professionals." "Working for wages need not preclude one from a substantial voice in organizational decisions and in setting educational policies" (Kerchner, 1992). While Kerchner is on the correct path, his optimism about the willingness of the public in general and school boards in particular to accept greater and more meaningful input from teachers has, thus far, little to no basis in historical precedent.

In the mid-1980s both the NEA and the AFT identified and publicized settings wherein changes in collective bargaining strategies, formal contractual agreements, and informal cooperative arrangements might simultaneously promote educational reforms and protect employee rights (Rauth, 1990; Rosow & Zager, 1989). Regardless of whether teacher unions acted in response to criticisms of self-centeredness and/or recalcitrance,

145

or to their diminished stature in governmental arenas and in genuine real-life problems confronting schools, they, unlike many entrenched organizations, were apparently willing to take on new roles and responsibilities (Bacharach, Shedd, & Conley, 1989; Johnson, 1988; McDonnell & Fuhrman, 1986). They were reportedly "embracing the opportunity and obligation to be advocates and allies of education reform as well as promoters and protectors of employee well-being" (Malen, 1994).

Whether it is ultimately possible to protect employee well-being while embracing reform is debatable. That changes in the present system of "schooling" are sought by numerous persons, from varied backgrounds, and with vastly differing ideas is not debatable. The form that any changes should take is altogether inconsistent, and in fact, often varies not only by degree but by substance. The tremendous variance in "reform" proposals may make practical the shelving of the entire debate in favor of a more practical debate on the local level concerning changes in given schools.

Is Teaching an Art, a Science, or a Calling?

The importance of "good" teaching is difficult to question. The problem for teaching as a "profession" is in coming to grips with the exact nature of what it is that "good" teachers do, and how "good" teaching as either a science, an art, or a combination of both can effectively be transmitted to prospective teachers. Wayne C. Booth (1988) describes teaching as "the most difficult and important of all the arts. Like all arts, it surely must depend in part on knowledge, but like all arts it depends on knowledge that is elusive, manifold, and resistant to clear formulation" (p. 210). Booth is not alone in his view that teaching is more art than science: "We are in sympathy with the general thrust of the notion that teaching is a craft rather than a science or discipline" (Holdaway, 1994, p. 208). Ann Lieberman and Lynne Miller

(1978) likewise believe that "the vague goals of teaching (such as individualize and teach everyone in the class), along with the ambiguous connection between what is taught and what is learned, require artistry, as opposed to scientific thought" (p. 56).

David T. Hansen (1994) moves beyond the art/science debate entirely to describe teaching in terms of the ancient religious and the more modern secular use of the word "vocation." To Hansen, teaching, rather than a choice of careers, is more in line with a "calling." "An individual who is strongly inclined toward teaching seems to be a person who is not debating whether to teach but rather is contemplating how or under what circumstances to do so" (Hansen, 1994, pp. 266-67). Hansen also acknowledges that many receive "the call" after beginning careers in other fields.

> To describe the inclination to teach as a budding vocation also calls attention to the person's sense of agency. It implies that he or she knows something about himself or herself, something important, valuable, worth acting upon. This suggests that one conceives of teaching as more than a job, as more than a way to earn an income...but as potentially meaningful, as the way to instantiate one's desire to contribute to and engage with the world. (Hansen, 1994, p. 267)

Is a "Calling" Compatible with "Professionalism?"

Educational researchers frequently compare teachers' work with the kinds of work performed in other occupations (Rowan, 1994). In these analyses, teaching is usually seen as a form of professional work, that is, a type of complex work requiring a great deal of specialized knowledge (*e.g.*, Sykes, 1990). However true it may be that teaching is complex, the widely accepted notion that teaching is, to some degree at least, a "calling," leads to the inescapable conclusion that comparisons to "accepted professions," such as law, are inappropriate at best.

While not my purpose to berate lawyers, it is relatively rare that a person enters law school to either "see justice done" or to "change society." According to the *ABA Journal* (September 1986), the reasons more than half of the practicing attorneys who responded to that particular poll recall being attracted to law school was because "the subject interested them" or "their work as lawyers would be interesting." Even less in line with a "calling," 46 percent said they chose law because of "income potential," and 43 percent listed the "prestige of a legal career" (See also Moll, 1990, p. 25).

However valid these notions, we might be disturbed if such numbers were true of teachers. How would teachers feel if 46 percent of their colleagues said they chose teaching because of "income potential?" More important than how teachers might feel, how would parents feel if income potential was known to be a prime motivator of those who became the teachers of their children?

Efforts to compare teaching with other occupations are often not efforts to logically analyze the professions, but are rather rooted in broader concerns about the professional status of teaching. Although education workers in the United States have been trying to professionalize the occupation of teaching since at least the turn of the century, most observers agree that this project has been only partially successful (Rowan, 1994). Aside from the limited success of the effort to "professionalize" teaching, there is a fairly significant debate over the value of the "professional" label itself. "Broad labels such as profession, craft, or labor often conceal as much as they reveal, especially when used to describe the nature of work performed by a given occupation" (Rowan, 1994, p. 5).

Others more simply believe that, whether or not teaching is a "true" profession, it is not (and will not be) viewed as a profession because the complexity of teaching is hidden beneath the apparent simplicity of its execution and because it is not cloaked in unfamiliar language (Goens & Glover, 1991; Bacharach, *et al.*, 1990). "As sociological research on work and occupations demonstrates, the prestige and earnings that accrue to an occupation depend to a significant extent on the complexity of the work performed by that occupation" (Rowan, 1994, p. 13).

Eliot Freidson (1986) similarly wrote about the "mystification of knowledge," pointing out that the established professions have been able to thrive through their own good fortune and their intentional and careful cultivation of an image. Such a "mystification of knowledge" that has accrued to the benefit of the legal and medical "professions" runs counter to the long-term goal of educators, which is and should be the de-mystification of knowledge. Seeking greater involvement in the education of children by parents and the community as a whole is almost universally seen as beneficial (see among others, Crowson, 1992; Wanat, *et al.*, 1994).

Teaching's claim to professional status is grounded in the following reality: Teaching children and adolescents is complex work, and successful performance of this work requires high levels of general educational development and specific vocational preparation (Rowan, 1994). Assuming we accept this, then the question is not whether teachers should be afforded the status of doctors and lawyers, but rather "what meaning should teachers and non-teachers alike attach to the profession of teaching?"

Does "Professionalism" Accrue Without Cost?

Assuming, as many do, that teaching will only be improved (however vague that term is) by its greater acceptance as a "profession" in line with the more established "professions," then will such improvement come without cost? There has been no shortage of literature about "professionalism," and if that literature is judged by its lack of real and measurable impact, it is arguable that too much has already been written about "professionalism" generally, and the "professionalization of teaching" specifically. By the mid to late 1980s, professionalism was becoming a tired subject for many education authors (*i.e.*, Ginsburg, 1987). Yet despite the "tiredness" of the subject, the value of the debate remains if only because the resolution of the problem has not yet arrived.

While much has been written extolling the virtues of "professionalism" and the term itself conjures up almost exclusively positive connotations, little has been written suggesting that the "need" to "professionalize" teaching comes at a significant cost. Notable among the few "doubters" has been William Ayers (1992) who warned of the dangers thusly: "if teachers see professionalism as a type of elitism separating them from the community at large, a successful 'partnership' among teachers, parents, administrators, and the community will be more difficult" (p. 24). While little argument exists among most members within the teaching profession who would presumably like to see the income and status of teachers raised, the impact of and subsequent dangers of seeking greater "professionalism," at least in terms of what "professionalism" has commonly meant, have been largely ignored. Foremost upon such a list of dangers lies the detachment requirement that "professionals" need to embody, and which their respective "professions" require.

Among many theorized dangers of "professionalization" are the tendency to serve the profession first, to believe the ideology, to utilize the mythology, to separate from the people, to mystify the knowledge, to protect secrets, to abuse power, and to avoid responsibility (Kraybill & Pellman Good, 1982; Andrews, 1992). While each of these elements may be harmful in themselves, perhaps the most relevant as far as teaching is concerned lies in the tendency of "professionals" to distance themselves from their work. Such distancing can come at the expense of creating quality personal relationships. It is such distancing, however appropriate in many professions, that is a potential danger within the teaching profession—at least insofar as the distance might hinder personal relationships that foster learning.

In seeking greater "professionalization" through attempts to compare teaching with the more commonly accepted "professions," there is a tendency to ignore the negative elements that might come along with the positive elements in the rush to achieve the status and recognition commonly afforded the more accepted professions. Since teaching kids and young adults is vastly different from performing surgery, diagnosing individual patient or client needs, and most, if not all other aspects of law and medicine, there should be a certain amount of trepidation that comes along with comparing "apples and oranges." So far, however, there has been little reluctance on the part of teachers and teachers' organizations toward proposing greater "professionalization." Such a full speed ahead approach has led to a diminishment in the analysis of any potential costs, as most of the literature simply compares and contrasts teaching with the more established professions, while largely ignoring the differences in the ultimate "product."

Lost for the most part in the desire to professionalize is the recognition that professionalism (at least in the traditional sense) would mean greater detachment. Such greater "professional" detachment is difficult to perceive of as better for students' needs. Many educators have ably focused upon the need for "attachment" and caring, as opposed to detachment. Ayers (1992) specifically decried professionalism if it were to mean "an overemphasis on developing a 'knowledge base' for teaching and a corresponding weakening of attributes like compassion" (p. 24). Mem Fox (1993) perhaps put it best:

> I see no age difference in the fundamental need for good relationships in teaching/learning situations; I believe they arise from knowing those whom we teach and knowing those who teach us: from being open about our lives and our own outside-school realities, and from caring about and knowing the different people in our classes. (p. 78)

While many of Mem Fox's reflections specifically concern reading, her thoughts are equally appropriate to learning in general. "I'm certain that learning to read and learning to love reading owe a great deal (more than we ever dreamed) to the nature of the human relationships that occur around and through books" (Fox, 1993, p. 136). It is the human relationships that occur between teacher and student that create within the student an interest in learning that might continue beyond the teacher-student contact. Just as parents attempt to instill within their children security, love, and independence, so too should teachers attempt to instill within their students the security of a good learning environment, love of the subject, and the independence to continue learning long after the class is over.

Success as a teacher must necessarily lie in fostering the human relationships in which the teacher and the student are allowed to follow their natural inclinations in a classroom. These natural inclinations usually follow the path of teacher as leader and students as followers of that lead. To effectively teach all our students requires that we acknowledge the differences between and among our students, and treat them as individuals that we care about. The detachment of the "professions" runs counter to such involvement.

School improvement requires systemic change in teacher improvement and equalized school capacity, not higher content and performance standards (Darling-Hammond, 1994). It is the "large inequalities in opportunities to learn that are more responsible for learning gaps than a paucity of tests" (Darling-Hammond, 1994, p. 478). Any attempts to increase the "opportunities to learn," aside from the useless rhetoric coming from Congress and most state legislatures, must at base focus upon teachers and their interactions with individual students.

Another potential pitfall of "copycat professionalism" lies in the difficulty accepted autonomous "professionals" often have in working together toward a common goal. "A profession that derives its authority and its influence from the fact that people need its services can become exploitative unless its members possess a high degree of altruism and work together to promote and foster high ideals in themselves and in their colleagues" (Curtin, 1994, p. 32). "Professionalism" for teachers depends in large part upon the trust that teachers are able to justifiably evoke from the parents of their students and from their students themselves. Anything less than this type of "caring professionalism," is inappropriate for teachers, if not morally, then simply because of the nature of their work.

Since "good teaching" is so difficult to define with any certainty, the ability of education detractors to bemoan the state of education and their accompanying pleas to overcome "poor teaching" and poor student outcomes continues to mount. Since we societally are reluctant to blame ourselves for the shortcomings, real or perceived, in others or often even ourselves, many have latched onto teachers as the scapegoats for poor educational outcomes, high drop-out rates, and a general and undefinable lessening in our "values." Because teachers are accessible and, as of yet, have not effectively raised their voices in outrage against such blame, they continue to be perceived not only as passive, but as accepting of the criticism as implied by their relative silence.

Many inside and outside of the education "establishment" have proposed "solutions" to the problems confronting teacher education programs. Whether these reformers feel a real need to overcome teacher deficiencies or merely to placate the public is debatable, but in any case, many proposals have been cast out to test the waters of public and legislative opinion. "Recent policy proposals for reforming teacher preparation have highlighted once again apparent limitations of teacher education and problems associated with initiation to teaching" (Holdaway, *et al.*, 1994, p. 205).

Proposals ranging from greater teacher autonomy to increasing and tightening standards to which teachers should be held allow for a wide variety of criticisms directed at schools generally and teachers primarily. Even those who generally are supportive of teachers often add to the assumption that teachers are doing a poor job through their proposals that aim at teachers, rather than at schools and/or the negative influences of poverty, crime, and other mountainous obstacles that many children face.

Blaming the teachers has been popular not only with critics on the "outside," but often with critics "inside" schools, colleges of education, and other would-be "teacher sympathizers." Suggestions such as internships for beginning teachers (even beyond required student-teaching experiences) do suggest a certain amount of fear of the damage that might be caused by beginning and inexperienced teachers. "Internships may play a significant role in developing competencies on the job and facilitating the transition from university student to full-fledged professional. By overcoming the disjunction between theoretical education and practical preparation, internship programs may ultimately prove to be an important vehicle for enhancing the quality of teaching" (Holdaway, _et al._, 1994, p. 219). Whether or not internships, as an example, would "improve" teaching, the implied assumption is that poor teaching is at the heart of the problems facing schools.

The Importance of "Micro-Reform"

The fact that situations differ radically across states, counties, school districts, and even within school districts, mandates that the debate focus on local schools and local problems. Just as microeconomics differs in form from macroeconomics, school reform discussion has centered on "macro-reform," while neglecting "micro-reform." This is not to deny the value of "macro-reform" discussion, it is only to suggest that a shift in effort towards "micro-reform" might serve a more practical and ultimately greater long-term benefit.

"Macro-reform," or reform in the aggregate, as I define it for these purposes, often bears great similarity to "micro-reform," as seen in the proposals for an "experimental school system" encompassing many districts in different areas as described by Dwight Allen (1992) in his book *Schools for a New Century*. This essay embraces the "concept" of experimental schools while dismissing it as unnecessary in an environment in which teachers lead reform by actively engaging the public in debate about the concerns of given schools.

So then, what is "micro-reform," and is it merely another "experiment" which should be met with a healthy dose of skepticism? "Micro-reform" is only a centering of the debate on the problems of a given, definable school district, and the ways in which the delivery of educational services might be improved in that district. The expectations that we can somehow develop a neat and tidy blueprint for the school of the future have been part of the problem limiting the success of any school reform. "The last thing we need is some modern-day managerial guru laying out another "single-best system" for overhauling the public schools" (Fiske, 1992, p. 15).

In the final analysis it is up to every school district, every school, every reader to decide which blend of the available elements is best for particular circumstances. That's what it means to be "smart" (Fiske, 1992, p. 15). A great irony in all of this lies in the federal government's increasing belief in "local control" and the subsequent justifications for lesser funding, while simultaneously promoting broad "reform" of public education.

Chapter Summary

Certain realities of our system of public schooling, such as the trend toward professionalization coupled with the compulsory attendance by students, force the consideration of issues such as accountability, freedom, and technocratization. The obsession with "professionalization" and the use of medicine and law as model professions is useless at best, and potentially harmful at worst. The reliance of the well grounded professions on a formal code of ethics and on the "mystification of knowledge" can result in inappropriate treatment of individuals. While the professions often have tremendous contact with their own culturally formed "self-righteousness," they often have less contact with what is "right" for individuals they "counsel."

Fenstermacher (1990) differentiates teaching from law and medicine on the grounds that (1) the mystification of knowledge is intrinsic to those two professions, while teaching is predicated on making knowledge accessible, and (2) those professions maintain social distance, while teaching, in contrast, needs to enhance social connection in order to be most effective, and (3) those professions model one-sided effort, while successful teaching is marked by a reciprocity of effort.

While teacher "empowerment" and teacher "professionalism" are no doubt worthy goals, they are, from the point of view of the system as a whole, limited ones. Do happy teachers make smarter kids? Common sense says that this follows, but the connection is yet to be demonstrated (Fiske, 1991, p. 58). Teachers should also be aware of the logical extension to their arguments in favor of greater "decentralization." "If the underlying premise is that 'stakeholders' in the educational enterprise should have a voice in running the system, then why not include parents? students? members of the community?" (Fiske, 1991, p. 58). While such inclusion has been within the realm of those pushing for greater micro-reform, there are potential implications for teacher professionalization, just as "community policing" has implications for increasing the professionalization of our police.

Michael F. DiPaola and Wayne K. Hoy (1994) conclude that:

> ...principals who want to cultivate a climate of professionalism and change in their schools should avoid reliance on bureau-

cratic authority to control teachers and instead nurture a professional teacher perspective of autonomy. Such an orientation may increase militancy and conflict, but the conflict and militancy produced by professional teacher action will likely lead to constructive change and help avoid rigidity and stagnation in schools. (p. 87)

Ultimately, while greater professionalism is appropriately pursued for many reasons, we will be better served by recognizing that proper professionalism for teachers and teaching must not embody "copycat professionalism" but an entirely new type of professionalism that acknowledges our necessary association with unionism as positive, not negative—one that encompasses much of what law and medicine have traditionally stood for, but also one in which many of the "requirements" of the more established professions are properly rejected.

Charles J. Sykes (1989) viewed the proper goal for teachers as not a position among the high professions, which he viewed as quite unlikely, but merely a more manageable improvement in their status. Jurgen Herbst (1989) similarly concludes that teachers "can and should develop their own professionalism, not an imitation of the professionalism of doctors, lawyers and school administrators, but through their own indigenous professional conduct in the classroom" (p. 196).

While all professions have their inconsistencies, teaching as a profession, at least in the traditional sense, is frought with them. Unlike teaching law or medicine, teaching education at the collegiate level seems to require previous experience teaching much younger children. Such an informal "internship" seems to run contrary to the "science" of the more traditional professions which allow "practice" after completion of satisfactory entrance examinations, without great regard, especially in the case of the law, to practical experience in the field. If teachers and teachers of teachers feel that their programs are more important than law or medicine, and therefore might require a satisfactory internship program to minimize potential harm to future students, then so be it. If that is the case however, then comparisons with law and medicine seem to be inappropriate.

Moreover, however easy it may be to simply compare teaching with law and medicine, and then attempt to validate such comparisons in the hope of attaining some of the status that the two more accepted "professions" have been afforded (both rightly and wrongly), it is wrongheaded and would ultimately be both disappointing for our students and less fulfilling for ourselves. One should only have to attend one conference in which many lawyers are gathered to conclude that "being more like lawyers is not in the best interests of teaching, or of students."

While exceptions to the generalization abound, "lawyer in America has come to connote egoism and rabid competitiveness coupled with greed, a seeming detachment from issues of right and wrong, and one who is very bright and hardworking but, so often, dull" (Moll, 1990, p. 3). If this is the "professional" model that teachers aspire to, they should pause and deliberate carefully, for after true "professionalism" is attained, it will take a long time for the student/teacher and teacher/parent relationships to adjust. The adjustment may well be more damaging in the long term than education can bear.

> The phenomenon of learning takes place in diverse ways, and we'd be fooling ourselves if we believed it happened only when we "teach" in the narrow sense. Our ultimate success as teachers can't really be measured until our students have left us. If, in their continuing lives, our past students can deal confidently and competently with any real (situation) only then can we claim to have taught them well. (Fox, 1993, p. 109)

Confidence and competence may best be instilled through positive teacher-student relationships, in which students feel certain that their teachers actually "care" about their success. In this age, when more and more students come to school carrying a heavy burden of social and emotional baggage, it is even more important that teachers not lose sight of their obligation to "care." Such an obligation should carry much greater status than our society has afforded teachers, but casting aside that obligation will do great and lasting harm to the "profession" of teaching, and more painfully still, to the students themselves.

The challenge in education is to find incentives that do not divide but bring about a collaborative search for better ways of coping with an extremely difficult set of problems (Bok, 1993, p. 192). Teachers should have more time to meet and discuss their work. As professionals, they should be full participants in deliberations over curriculum, teaching methods, and other questions of academic policy (Bok, 1993). If schools are in such a state generally that we have reached consensus on the need for "reform," then let the teachers lead the charge in the interests of their students and themselves in search of appropriate reform. Such leadership and such a call to action has at least as great a chance for success as any of the recent calls for inaction couched in the terms of "professionalism."

Chapter Eight
Conclusions

"Preventative Educational Reform" vs. "Attention to Symptoms"

Ultimately, it is how the debate is shaped that determines which direction any real educational or political reform might take. In carrying through the health-care analogy, at the moment this debate seems to concern the sweeping proposals of those in favor of "preventative educational reform" and "major political reform" vs. the less inclusive, less ambitious, "band-aid solutions" or "attention to symptoms" proposals from those seeking to first stop the bleeding in areas hardest hit, and/or to address only the most aggregious campaign abuses, while refusing to consider overhaul of the entire campaign system which so ably encourages those same abuses.

Usually the term "band-aid" solution has suffered from negative implications and the perception that those proposing the "band-aids" do so in lieu of offering real and lasting improvement. In the context of political reform, "band-aid" solutions seem to deserve their negative image. In the context of school reform, however, it is time to first apply the band-aids and "stop the bleeding" in those districts in which the suffering is great, and only after the bleeding is stopped, might we look toward and encourage real "reform" in any holistic and preventative sense.

The value of a "triage" approach again lies in the eyes of the beholder. Among those in districts where "bleeding" is occurring, such an approach would no doubt be viewed favorably. In districts with adequate wealth which begets adequate school resources, and with relatively little "bleeding," attention to others might likely be viewed unfavorably. It is time, however, to stop trying to please everyone through widespread "school reform" and instead focus on "reforming" schools and educational areas that truly need help.

It is within the power of every school and district to make the continuous improvements in excellence and equity that add up to educational reform. "Continuous improvements require systemic changes in the ways that schools and districts operate — changes made with the active support of management, teachers, and teachers' unions" (Rosow & Zager, 1989, p. 92). We need not, nor could we, impose a blanket set of reforms that would improve all schools. When we as a society come to fully realize that fact, which seems so painfully obvious, we will then be able to properly shift our focus to reforms that really do matter, in places that really do need some intervention.

To heighten the credibility of the debate on school choice, "family values," and other "virtues" extolled by William Bennett and Rush Limbaugh, among others, is yet another insult to those with the fewest advantages in our society. If society is becoming less virtuous, and reform is needed, it is not particularly virtuous to preach that those in possession of life preservers should bail out and not turn back to look at those aboard what the "survivors" consider a sinking public education system.

Let us attempt to stop the bleeding and tend to the sick,

before we declare that a new system is warranted and a new start is necessary. Only then will any new start or new system have any acceptable level of fairness, and only then can any plan to increase the "virtue" of our children be undertaken by our public schools and, ultimately, by our society. In looking carefully and critically at all proposals, and perhaps most importantly, the agenda of those espousing given reform proposals, we may see that all of our "best interests are served" by first stopping the bleeding within our schools prior to setting course on widespread "reform."

> We all know Bennett's thirty-dollar placebos are useless, that people buy them because they make them feel better, that they represent not the world we live in but the one some of us wish we did. We also know that the kids most in need of hope and uplifting will never get near a William Bennett hardcover and would run screaming in horror if they did. The joke is on us, but it isn't funny—our children will have to make their way through the new culture and technology as best they can, apparently with little sane help from us. (Katz, 1997, p. 34)

The debate over whether to teach "virtue" in the schools is as misguided as the debate over what makes up a "family." The tendency our society has had toward an oversimplification and the subsequent division into two sides as we consider issues, is addressed by James Q. Wilson (1993) who believes that the argument over teaching children morality is neither conservative nor liberal.

> Children do not learn morality by learning maxims or clarifying values. They enhance their natural sentiments by being regularly induced by families, friends, and institutions to behave in accord with the most obvious standards of right conduct—fair dealing, reasonable self-control, and personal honesty. A moral life is perfected by practice more than by precept; children are not taught so much as habituated. (p. 249)

Neil Postman (1995) expresses his belief that there are numerous ways in which to learn and none can be viewed as superior to the rest. "There is no one who can say that this or that is the best way to know things, to feel things, to see things, to remember things, to apply things, to connect things and that no other will do as well. In fact, to make such a claim is to trivialize learning, to reduce it to mechanical skill" (p. 3).

Trivializing learning is at the heart of "instilling" the virtues of some upon all of our children. Given the outside and inside influences upon our children, it is more important than ever that schoolteachers and those associated with the education of our youth practice what they preach.

There's Trouble Right Here in River City, But Should We Form a Band?

Our rising expectations of quality in education probably have exceeded our actual accomplishments. When this occurs, there is usually a sense of despair. But feelings of frustration and despair should not be permitted to obscure the genuine achievements in schooling during the last eight to nine decades. Moreover, we know that impatience associated with the progress of reform is heightened when the possibility of complete fulfillment of reform goals is within view. Our nation is experiencing such an impatience as demonstrated by publication of the many different reports on educational reform. (Willie & Miller, 1988, p. 4)

Impatience alone, however, is not sufficient cause for widespread reform. More important than succumbing to impatient desires to reform, we need to pause to consider who, for the most part, is behind the impatience with the present system of public education. Many of the "virtuous" who say public education is failing us, like former Secretary of Education William Bennett, have a history of clear agendas set forth to advance private education. Many others are not convinced that public education is at the root of the problem whatever the problem is, and remain reluctant to jump aboard any vehicle headed for reform.

No matter where our sympathies lie, before we continue blindly jumping on the bandwagon that is "educational reform," it is at least worthwhile to consider who is driving the bandwagon, and whether the drivers might be leading us to a place where they want us to go more than where we need to go. It is with that caveat that we should look at the bandwagon not as a school bus, but rather as an ambulance. As an ambulance, it should be sent out first to those who need it the most.

If any real comprehensive reform is to occur, we must first and foremost stop the bleeding. Unfortunately, our system for supporting the education of young people comes close to modeling the attributes of our economic system, which is, in effect, a sort of "reverse triage."

> It gives the best schooling to the children who already have the advantage of parents who had such schooling and the worst schooling to children whose parents are poor and ill-schooled. In effect, it is a system for throwing money at the rich to make their kids richer. And these characteristics are undergirded by the high percentage of its support from state and local taxes, which are much more regressive than federal taxes, so that the costs of schools fall more heavily on the lower income groups in America, even as their children are less well served than those in wealthier districts. (Howe, 1993, p. 111)

Much of the "virtue" debate and dialogue excludes those who don't "belong." Lisa Delpit (1995) refers to the "silenced dialogue" that often occurs when persons who feel unheard simply stop talking, not as a form of agreement, but rather as a form of self-preservation (p. 21). Being left out of the dialogue, particularly a dialogue controlled and dominated by confident, if not arrogant, and powerful ideologues, must surely be among the great frustrations of human existence.

As always, talk is cheap. Advocating "virtue" is easy. The difficult part lies in actually changing behavior of the people who influence children. Thomas J. Lasley (1997) advocates the achievement of this goal by making it clear that "people matter and need to be taken seriously and respected." It seems self-evident that we need to compare the words with the deeds of influential persons such as Limbaugh and Bennett as a way of tempering the influence that these persons or any person might have upon establishing "virtue." "Respect for people" is not, seemingly at least, among the most obvious traits of Limbaugh and Bennett. It seems as though those who preach for greater virtue should see in themselves a logical starting point for practicing greater virtue.

References

Adler, M.J. (1977). *Reforming Education*. New York: MacMillan.

Ahrne, G. (1994). *Social Organizations: Interaction inside, outside and between organizations*. London, United Kingdom: Sage.

Allen, D.W. (1992). *Schools for a New Century: A conservative approach to radical school reform*. New York: Praeger.

Alter, J. (1994a, October 3). The Record Nobody Knows. *Newsweek*, 49.

Alter, J. (1994b, October 17). Day of the Hyenas. *Newsweek*, 41

American Psychological Association, Commission on Violence and Youth. (1993). *Violence and Youth: Psychology's Response*, Volume 1 (Summary Report). Washington, DC: American Psychological Association.

Andrews, D. (1992, October). Beyond the Professionalisation of Community Work. *Social Alternatives*, *11*(3), 35-38.

Asimov, I. (1987, April 23). Jennings Koppel Report: Memo to the Future, ABC News, transcript, 12.

Astor, R.A. (1995, April). School Violence: A Blueprint for Elementary School Interventions. *Social Work in Education*, *17*(2), 101-115.

Ayers, W. (1992). Work That is Real: Why Teachers Should Be Empowered. In G.A. Hess, Jr. (Ed.), *Empowering Teachers and Parents*. Westport, CT: Bergin & Garvey, 13-28.

Bacharach, S., Shedd, J., & Conley, S. (1989). School Management and teacher unions: The capacity for cooperation in an age of reform. *Teachers College Record, 91,* 97-105.

Bacharach, S.B., Bamberger, P., Conley, S.C., & Bauer, S. (1990, May). The Dimensionality of Decision Participation in Educational Organizations: The Value of a Multi-Domain Evaluative Approach. *Educational Administration Quarterly, 26*(2), 126-167.

Barash, D.P. (1992). *The L Word.* New York: William Morrow.

Baskin, M.G., & Thomas, L.M. (1986). School metal detector searches. *University of Michigan Journal of Law Reform, 19,* 1037-1106.

Berliner, D.C., & Biddle, B.J. (1995). *The Manufactured Crisis: Myths, Fraud, and the Attack on America's Public Schools.* Reading: MA: Addison-Wesley.

Bok, D. (1993). *The Cost of Talent.* New York: The Free Press.

Booth, W.C. (1988). *The Vocation of a Teacher.* Chicago, IL: The University of Chicago Press.

Bork, R.H. (1996). *Slouching Towards Gomorrah: Modern Liberalism and American Decline.* New York: HarperCollins.

Bourgois, P. (1995). Poverty and Unemployment Cause Crime. In D. Bender & B. Leone (Eds.), *Crime and Criminals: Opposing Viewpoints.* San Diego, CA: Greenhaven Press, 46-51.

Brace, P., & Hinckley, B. (1992). *Follow the Leader.* New York: Basic Books.

Campbell, C. (1996). Management in a Sandbox: Why the Clinton White House Failed to Cope with Gridlock. In C. Campbell & B.A. Rockman (Eds.), *The Clinton Presidency: First Appraisals.* Chatham, NJ: Chatham House, 51-87.

Carter, J. (1992). *Turning Point.* New York: Times Books.

Carter, J. (1996). *Living Faith.* New York: Times Books.

Caudle, M. (1994, September). Why Can't Johnny Be Safe? Eliminating School Violence. *The High School Magazine, 2,* 10-13.

Chomsky, N. (1991). *Deterring Democracy.* New York: Hill & Wang.

Clabaugh, G.K. (1994, Winter). Reflections on School Disorder. *Educational Horizons, 72*(2), 61-63.

Clinton, H.R. (1996). *It Takes a Village: And Other Lessons Children Teach Us.* New York: Simon & Schuster.

Coleman, J.S., Campbell, E., Hobson, C., McPartland, J., Mood, A., Weinfield, F., & York, R. (1966). *Equality of Educational Opportunity.* Washington, DC: U.S. Government Printing Office.

Connell, R.W. (1994, Summer). Poverty and Education, *Harvard Educational Review, 64*(2), 125-149.

Crowson, R.L. (1992). *School-community Relations Under Reform.* Berkeley, CA: McCutchan.

Cuban, L. (1992). Policies for Public Schooling in the 1990s. In J.A. Pechman & M.S. McPherson (Eds.), *Fulfilling America's Promise.* Ithaca, NY: Cornell University Press, 25-49.

Cuomo, M. (1995). *Reason to Believe.* New York: Simon & Schuster.

Currie, E. (1995). The Culture of Social Irresponsibility Causes Crime. In D. Bender & B. Leone, (Eds.), *Crime and Criminals: Opposing Viewpoints*, (59-66). San Diego, CA: Greenhaven Press.

Curtin, L.L. (1994, August). Collegial Ethics of a Caring Profession. *Nursing Management, 25*(8), 28-32.

Darling-Hammond, L. (1994, August). National Standards and Assessments: Will They Improve Education? *American Journal of Education, 102*(4), 478-510.

Darling-Hammond, L., & Snyder, J. (1992). Reframing Accountability: Creating learner-centered schools. In A. Leiberman (Ed.), *The Changing Contexts of Teaching. Ninety-first Yearbook of the National Society for the Study of Education* (Part 1). Chicago, IL: National Society for the Study of Education, 11-36.

Delpit, L. (1995). *Other People's Children: Cultural Conflict in the Classroom.* New York: The New Press.

Denton, R.E., Jr., (1988). *The Primetime Presidency of Ronald Reagan.* New York: Praeger Publishers.

DiPaola, M.F., & Hoy, W.K. (1994, Winter). Teacher Militancy: A Professional Check on Bureaucracy. *The Journal of Research and Development in Education, 27*(2), 83-88.

Doyle, D.P., & Cooper, B.S. (Eds.), (1988). *Federal Aid to the Disadvantaged, What Future for Chapter 1?* Bristol, PA: The Falmer Press.

Driscoll, M.E. (1995). Thinking Like a Fish: The Implications of the Image of School Community for Connections between Parents and Schools. In P.W. Cookson, Jr. & B. Schneider (Eds.), *Transforming Schools.* New York: Garland, 209-236.

Dubos, R. (1962). *The Torch of Life.* New York: Pocket Books.

Duncan, B.J. (1997, Winter). Character Education: Reclaiming the Social. *Educational Theory, 47*(1), 119-130.

Eastland, T. (1992, September). Rush Limbaugh: Talking Back. *Ameri-*

can Spectator, 25(9), 22-27.

Edelman, M.W. (1992). *The Measure of our Success*. Boston, MA: Beacon Press.

Edsall, T.B. (1984). *The New Politics of Inequality*. New York: W.W. Norton.

Edwards III, G.C. (1996). Frustration and Folly: Bill Clinton and The Public Presidency. In C. Campbell & B.A. Rockman (Eds.), *The Clinton Presidency: First Appraisals*. Chatham, NJ: Chatham House, 234-261.

Ehrenreich, B. (1989). *Fear of Falling*. New York: HarperCollins.

Ehrenreich, B. (1990). *The Worst Years of Our Lives*. New York: Pantheon Books.

Elam, S. (1995). The Chameleon's Dish, Promise-Crammed. In D.R. Walling (Ed.), *At the Threshold of the Millenium*. Bloomington, IN: Phi Delta Kappa Educational Foundation, 23-31.

Elam, S.M., Rose, L.C., & Gallup, A.M. (1996, September). The 28th Annual Phi Delta Kappan/Gallup Poll of the Public's Attitudes Toward the Public Schools. *Phi Delta Kappan*, 78(1), 41-59.

Engvall, R.P. (1995). Public Sector Unionization in 1995: It Appears the Lion King Has Eaten Robin Hood. *Journal of Collective Negotiations in the Public Sector*, 24(3), 255-269.

Etzioni, A. (1993). *The Spirit of Community: The Reinvention of American Society*. New York: Touchstone Books.

Evans, W.H., & Evans, S.S. (1985). The Assessment of School Violence. *Pointer*, 29, 18-21.

Feder, J. (1985). *An Investigation of the Perceived Effects of Assault on Classroom Teachers*. New York: New York University Press.

Fenstermacher, G.D. (1990). Some Moral Considerations on Teaching as a Profession. In J.I. Goodlad, R. Soder, & K.S. Sirotnik (Eds.), *The Moral Dimensions of Teaching*. San Francisco, CA: Jossey-Bass Publishers, 130-154.

Feschbach, N.D., & Feschbach, S. (1982). Empathy training and the regulation of aggression. *Academic Psychology Bulletin*, 4, 393-413.

Fine, M. (1995). *Habits of Mind: Struggling Over Values in America's Classrooms*. San Francisco, CA: Jossey-Bass.

Fiske, E.B. (1991). *Smart Schools, Smart Kids*. New York: Simon & Schuster.

Fox, M. (1993). *Radical Reflections:Passionate Opinions on Teaching, Learning, and Living*. San Diego, CA: Harcourt Brace.

Freedman, J.O. (1996). *Idealism and Liberal Education*. Ann Arbor, MI: University of Michigan Press.

Freidson, E. (1986). *Professional Powers*. Chicago, IL: The University of Chicago Press.

Frum, D. (1994). *Dead Right*. New York: Basic Books.

Furman, G.H. (1994, August). Outcome-Based Education and Accountability. *Education and Urban Society, 26*(4), 417-437.

Galbraith, J.K. (1992). *The Contented Majority*. Boston, MA: Houghton Mifflin.

Galbraith, J.K. (1992). *The Culture of Contentment*. Boston, MA: Houghton Mifflin.

Galbraith, J.K. (1996). *The Good Society*. Boston, MA: Houghton Mifflin Company.

Gardner, H. (1991). *The Unschooled Mind*. New York: BasicBooks.

Gingrich, N. (1995, July 24). Speech presented in Waterloo, IA. As reported in *The Daily Iowan*.

Ginsburg, M. (1987). Reproduction, Contradiction, and Conceptions of Professionalism: The Case of Pre-Service Teachers. In T. Popkewitz (Ed.), *Critical Studies in Teacher Education*. Philadelphia, PA: The Falmer Press, 86-129.

Glazer, N. (1988). *The Limits of Social Policy*. Cambridge, MA: Harvard University Press.

Glickman, C.D. (1993). *Renewing America's Schools: A Guide For School-Based Action*. San Francisco, CA: Jossey-Bass.

Goens, G.A., & Clover, S.I.R. (1991). *Mastering School Reform*. Boston, MA: Allyn & Bacon.

Goldfield, M. (1987). *The Decline of Organized Labor in the United States*. Chicago, IL: The University of Chicago Press.

Goldstein, A.P., Apter, S.J., & Harootunion, B. (1984). *School Violence*. Englewood Cliffs, NJ: Prentice-Hall.

Goodson, I.F. (1995). The Context of Cultural Inventions: Learning and Curriculum. In P.W. Cookson & B. Schneider (Eds.), *Transforming Schools*. New York: Garland, 307-327.

Goodwin, R.N. (1992). *Promises to Keep*. New York: Times Books.

Gottfredson, G.D., & Gottfredson, D.C. (1985). *Victimization in Schools*. New York: Plenum Press.

Greenfield, M. (1993, March 1). The New Straight Talk. *Newsweek*, 82.

Greenfield, M. (1997, April 21). A Word on "Standing." *Newsweek*, 86.

Greenstein, F.I. (1993-94, Winter). The Presidential Leadership Style of Bill Clinton: An Early Appraisal. *Political Science Quarterly*, *108*(4), 589-601.

Greider, W. (1981, December). The Education of David Stockman. *The Atlantic*, 248(6), 27-54.

Greider, W. (1992, November/December). Stand and Deliver. *Utne Reader*, 73-79. Reprinted from *Rolling Stone* (August 20, 1992).

Gutmann, A. (1987). *Democratic Education*. Princeton, NJ: Princeton University Press.

Haberman, M. (1994, Spring). Gentle Teaching in a Violent Society. *Educational Horizons*, 72(3), 131-135.

Hafner, A.L., & Ulanoff, S.H. (1994, August). Validity Issues and Concerns for Assessing English Learners. *Education and Urban Society*, *26*(4), 367-389.

Hagstrom, J. (1988). *Beyond Reagan: The New Landscape of American Politics*. New York: W.W. Norton.

Haller, H.B., & Norpoth, H. (1994, August). Let the Good Times Roll: The Economic Expectations of U.S. Voters. *American Journal of Political Science*, *38*(3), 625-650.

Handler, J.F. (1994, Fall). "Ending Welfare as we Know it"—Wrong for Welfare, Wrong for Poverty. *Georgetown Journal on Fighting Poverty*, *2*(1), 3-55.

Hansen, D.T. (1994, Summer). Teaching and the Sense of Vocation. *Educational Theory*, *44*(3), 259-275.

Harrington, M. (1962). *The Other America; Poverty in the United States*. New York: Macmillan.

Harrington, M. (1984). *The New American Poverty*. New York: Holt, Rinehart & Winston.

Herbst, J. (1989). *And Sadly Teach: Teacher Education and Profes-sionalization in American Culture*. Madison, WI: University of Wisconsin Press.

Herrnstein, R.J. & Murray, C.A. (1994). *The Bell Curve: Intelligence and Class Structure in American Life*. New York: The Free Press.

Hirsch, E.D., Jr. (1996). *The Schools We Need: & Why We Don't Have Them*. New York: Doubleday.

Hirschi, T. (1972). *Causes of Delinquency*. Berkeley, CA: University of California Press.

Hoffer, E. (1951). *The True Believer*. Alexandria, VA: Time-Life Books.

Holdaway, E.A., Johnson, N.A., Ratsoy, E.W., & Friesen, D. (1994, Summer). The Value of an Internship Program for Beginning Teachers. *Educational Evaluation and Policy Analysis, 16*(2), 205-221.

Horner, J.J. (1993). Disciplinary Hearings and Due Process. In *The Principal's Legal Handbook*. Topeka, KS: National Organization on Legal Problems of Education, 37-42.

Howe, H. (1993). *Thinking About Our Kids*. New York: The Free Press.

Hoy, W.K., & Tarter, C.J. (1993). A Normative Theory of Participative Decision Making in Schools. *Journal of Educational Administration, 31*(3), 4-19.

Hughes, R. (1993). *The Culture of Complaint: The Fraying of America*. New York: Oxford University Press.

Hunter, J.D. (1991). *The Culture Wars*. New York: Basic Books.

Ianni, F.A.J. (1978). The Social Organization of the High School: School Specific Aspects of School Crime. In E. Wenk & N. Harlow (Eds.), *School Crime and Disruption*. Davis, CA: Responsible Action of Davis, 21-36.

Ingersoll, R.M. (1994, Summer). Organizational Control in Secondary Schools, *Harvard Educational Review, 64*(2), 150-172.

Johnson, S.M. (1988, June). Pursuing Professional Reform in Cincinnati. *Phi Delta Kappan,* 69(10), 746-751.

Jones, C.O. (1996). Campaigning to Govern: The Clinton Style. In C. Campbell & B.A. Rockman (Eds.), *The Clinton Presidency: First Appraisals*. Chatham, NJ: Chatham House, 15-50.

Jourdan, J. (1994). A Community's Answer to Teen Violence. *Children Today, 23*(2), 20-24.

Katz, J. (1997). *Virtuous Reality*. New York: Random House.

Katznelson, I., & Weir, M. (1985). *Schooling For All*. New York: Basic Books.

Kerchner, C.T. (1992, March). Inventing Professional Unionism. Address delivered to the National Education Association National Conference, Portland, OR.

Kinsley, M. (1994, November 28). Money Talks. *New Republic,* 20-21, 24.

Kipper, B. (1996, June). Law Enforcement's Role in Addressing School Violence. *The Police Chief,* 63(6), 26-31.

Kirst, M.W. (1988, January). Who Should Control Our Schools? *NEA Today,* (Issues 88) *6,* 74-79.

Klein, J. (1994, November 14). An Awful Year. *Newsweek,* 39.

Kluegel, J.R. & Smith, E.R. (1981). Stratification Beliefs. *Annual*

Review of Sociology, 7, 29-56.

Kohn, A. (1986). *No Contest: The Case Against Competition*. Boston, MA: Houghton Mifflin.

Kohn, A. (1997, February). How Not to Teach Values: A Critical Look at Character Education. *Phi Delta Kappan, 78*(6), 429-439.

Korbin, J.E. (1992, January/February). Introduction: Child Poverty in the United States. *The American Behavioral Scientist, 35*, 213-219.

Kozol, J. (1995). *Amazing Grace: The Lives of Children and the Conscience of a Nation*. New York: Crown.

Kozol, J. (1991). *Savage Inequalities*. New York: Crown.

Kraybill, D., & Pellman Good, P. (Eds.). (1982). *Perils of Professionalism*. Scottdale, AZ: Herald Press.

Krosnick, J.A., & Brannon, L.A. (1993). The Media and the Foundations of Presidential Support: George Bush and the Persion Gulf Conflict. *Journal of Social Issues, 49*(4), 167-182.

Krugman, P. (1990). *The Age of Diminished Expectations*. Cambridge, MA: MIT Press.

Kuttner, R. (1997). *Everything For Sale: The Virtues and Limits of Markets*. New York: Alfred A. Knopf.

Kyvig, D.E. (1995, Fall/Winter). Refining or Resisting Modern Government? The Balanced Budget Amendment to the U.S. Constitution. *Akron Law Review, 28*(2), 97-124.

Lapham, L.H. (1993). *The Wish for Kings: Democracy at Bay*. New York: Grove Press.

Lasch, C. (1995). *The Revolt of the Elites: And the Betrayal of Democracy*. New York: W.W. Norton.

Lasley, T.J. (1997, April). The Missing Ingredient in Character Education. *Phi Delta Kappan, 78*(8), 654-655.

Leach, P. (1994). *Children First*. New York: Alfred A. Knopf.

Lekachman, R. (1982). *Greed Is Not Enough: Reaganomics*. New York: Pantheon Books.

Lieberman, A., & Miller, L. (1978, September). The Social Realities of Teaching. *Teachers College Record, 80*(1), 54-68.

Lightfoot, S.L. (1983). *The Good High School: Portraits of Character and Culture*. New York: Basic Books.

Limbaugh, R. (1992). *The Way Things Ought to Be*. New York: Pocket Books.

Lipset, S.M., & Schneider, W. (1983). *The Confidence Gap*. New York: Free Press.

Lloyd, T. (1994, Spring). Gordon, Griffin, and Clintonomics. *Contention*, *3*, 95-107.

Malen, B. (1994, February). Review of *A Union of Professionals: Labor Relations and Educational Reform*. *Educational Administration Quarterly*, *30*(1), 106-112.

Mayhew, L.B., Ford, P.J., & Hubbard, D.L. (1990). *The Quest for Quality: The Challenge for Undergraduate Education in the 1990s*. San Francisco, CA: Jossey-Bass Publishers.

McDonnell, L. & Fuhrman, S. (1986). The Political Context of Reform. In V.D. Mueller & M.P. McKeown (Eds.), *The Fiscal, Legal and Political Aspects of State Reform of Elementary and Secondary Education*. Cambridge, MA: Ballinger, 43-64.

McElvaine, R.S. (1987). *The End of the Conservative Era*. New York: Pantheon Books.

Meier, D. (1995). *The Power of Their Ideas: Lessons for America from a Small School in Harlem*. Boston, MA: Beacon Press.

Meilaender, G.C. (1984). *The Theory and Practice of Virtue*. Notre Dame, IN: The University of Notre Dame Press.

Messner, S.F., & Rosenfeld, R. (1997). *Crime and the American Dream* (2nd Ed.). Belmont, CA: Wadsworth.

Moll, R.W. (1990). *The Lure of the Law*. New York: Viking.

Monk, D.H. (1992). Education Productivity Research: An Update and Assessment of Its Role in Education Finance Reform. *Educational Evaluation and Policy Analysis*, *14*, 307-332.

Murphy, J., & Schiller, J. (1992). *Transforming America's Schools*. LaSalle, IL: Open Court.

National Commission on Excellence in Education. (1983). *A Nation at Risk: The Imperative for Educational Reform*. Washington, DC: U.S. Government Printing Office.

Natriello, G., McDill, E.L., & Pallas, A.M. (1990). *Schooling Disadvantaged Children: Racing Against Catastrophe*. New York: Teachers College Press.

Newman, K.S. (1993). *Declining Fortunes: The Withering of the American Dream*. New York: Basic Books.

Nisbet, R. (1990). *The Quest for Community: A Study in the Ethics of Order & Freedom*. San Francisco, CA: Institute for Contemporary Studies.

Nissani, M. (1994). Conceptual Conservatism: An Understated Variable in Human Affairs? *The Social Science Journal, 31*(3), 307-318.

Noguera, P.A. (1995, Summer). Preventing and Producing Violence: A Critical Analysis of Responses to School Violence. *Harvard Educational Review, 65*(2), 189-212.

O'Donoghue, J. (1995). Violence in the Schools. In L.L. Adler & F.L. Denmark (Eds.), *Violence and the Prevention of Violence* (101-108). Westport, CT: Praeger.

O'Reilly, R.C., & Green, E.T. (1992). *School Law For the 1990s: A Handbook*. Westport, CT: Greenwood Press.

Ornstein, A. (Winter 1995). The New Paradigm in Research on Teaching. *The Educational Forum, 59*(2), 124-129.

Perkins, D. (1992). *Smart Schools*. New York: The Free Press.

Peterson, P.E., & Rom, M. (1988). Lower Taxes, More Spending, and Budget Deficits. In C.O. Jones (Ed.), *The Reagan Legacy: Promise and Performance* (213-240). Chatham, NJ: Chatham House.

Phillips, K. (1990). *The Politics of Rich and Poor*. New York: Random House.

Phillips, K. (1994). *Arrogant Capital*. Boston, MA: Little Brown.

Plotkin, S., & Scheuerman, W.E. (1994). *Private Interest, Public Spending*. Boston, MA: South End Press.

Poole, R. (1991). *Morality and Modernity*. London, United Kingdom: Routledge.

Postman, N. (1995). *The End of Education: Redefining the Value of School*. New York: Alfred A. Knopf.

Pratkanis, A., & Aronson, E. (1992). *Age of Propaganda: The Everyday Use and Abuse of Persuasion*. New York: W.H. Freeman.

Rauth, M. (1990, June). Exploring Heresy in Collective Bargaining and School Restructuring. *Phi Delta Kappan, 71*(10), 781-790.

Reeves, R. (1985). *The Reagan Detour*. New York: Simon & Schuster.

Reich, R.B. (1989). *The Resurgent Liberal*. New York: Times Books.

Revel, J.F. (1991). *The Flight from Truth: The Reign of Deceit in the Age of Information*. New York: Random House.

Riley, R.W. (1994, January). Curbing Youth Violence. *USA Today Magazine of the American Scene, 122*(2584), 36-37.

Rockman, B.A. (1988). Conclusions: An Imprint but Not a Revolution. In B.B. Kymlicka & J.V. Matthews (Eds.), *The Reagan Revolution?* Chicago, IL: The Dorsey Press, 191-206.

Rockman, B.A. (1996). Leadership Style and the Clinton Presidency. In C. Campbell & B.A. Rockman (Eds.), *The Clinton Presidency: First*

Appraisals. Chatham, NJ: Chatham House, 325-362.

Rorty, A.O. (1993). Moral Imperialism vs. Moral Conflict: Conflicting Aims of Education. In B. Darling-Smith (Ed.), *Can Virtue Be Taught?* Notre Dame, IN: University of Notre Dame Press, 33-51.

Rosow, J.M., Zager, R. (1989). *Allies in Educational Reform: How Teachers, Unions, and Administrators Can Join Forces for Better Schools*. San Francisco, CA: Jossey-Bass Publishers.

Rowan, B. (1994, August-September). Comparing Teachers' Work with Work in Other Occupations: Notes on the Professional Status of Teaching. *Educational Researcher, 23*(6), 4-17,21.

Rozycki, E.G. (1994, Winter). School Violence, Punishment, and Justice. *Educational Horizons, 72*(2), 86-94.

Russell, B. (1977). *Education and the Social Order*. London, United Kingdom: Allen & Unwin.

Samuelson, R.J. (1994, October 24). Sowing More Cynicism. *Newsweek*, 45.

Sautter, R.C. (1995, January). Standing Up to Violence. *Phi Delta Kappan, 76*(5), K1-K12.

Schlesinger, A. (1992). *The Disuniting of America*. New York: W.W. Norton.

Scott, J.W. (1996). Academic Freedom as an Ethical Practice. In L. Menand (Ed.), *The Future of Academic Freedom*. Chicago, CA: The University of Chicago Press, 163-180.

Seron, C., & Ferris, K. (1995, February). Negotiating Professionalism. *Work and Occupations, 22*(1), 22-47.

Shames, L. (1991). *The Hunger for More: Searching for Values in an Age of Greed*. New York: Vintage Books.

Shanker, A. (1994-95, Winter). Privileging Violence: Too Much Focus on the Needs and "Rights" of Disruptive Students. *American Educator, 18*(4), 7.

Shields, J. (1995, Summer). Getting Corporations off the Public Dole. *Business and Society Review*, 94, 4-8.

Simon, H.A. (1957). *Models of Man*. New York: Wiley.

Simon, H.A., & Stedry, A.C. (1968). Psychology and economics. In G. Lindzey & E. Aronson (Eds.), *Handbook of Social Psychology*. Reading, MA: Addison-Wesley, 5, 269-314.

Sizer, T.R. (1992). *Horace's School*. Boston, MA: Houghton-Mifflin.

Smart, B. (1995). The subject of responsibility. *Philosophy & Social Criticism*, 21(4), 93-109.

Smith, R.B. (1997, March/April). Ideology, Partisanship, and the New

Political Continuum. *Society*, 34(3), 13-18.

Soder, R. (1990). The Rhetoric of Teacher Professionalization. In J.I. Goodlad, R. Soder, & K.S. Sirotnik (Eds.). *The Moral Dimensions of Teaching*. San Francisco, CA: Jossey-Bass, 296-328.

Sorensen, T.C. (1996). *Why I Am a Democrat*. New York: Henry Holt.

Sowell, T. (1995). *The Vision of the Annointed*. New York: Basic Books.

Spring, J. (1988). *Conflict of Interests: The Politics of American Education*. White Plains, NY: Longman.

Stanley, H.W. (1996). The Parties, the President, and the 1994 Midterm Elections. In C. Campbell & B.A. Rockman (Eds.), *The Clinton Presidency: First Appraisals*. Chatham, NJ: Chatham House, 188-211.

Starr, J. (1989). The Great Textbook War. In H. Holtz, *et al* (Eds.), *Education and the American Dream: Conservatives, Liberals, and Radicals Debate the Future of Education*. Granby, MA: Bergin & Garvey, 96-113.

Stone, F.M., & Boundy, K.B. (1994). School Violence: The Need for a Meaningful Response. *Clearinghouse Review* (Special Issue), 453-465.

Sykes, G. (1989). Teaching and Professionalism: A Cautionary Perspective. In L. Weis, P.G. Altbach, G.P. Kelly, H.G. Petrie, & S. Slaughter (Eds.), *Crisis in Teaching: Perspectives on Current Reforms*. Albany, NY: State University of New York Press, 253-273.

Sykes, G. (1990). Fostering Teacher Professionalism in Schools. In R.F. Elmore *et al.*, *Restructuring Schools: The Next Generation of Educational Reform*. San Francisco, CA: Jossey Bass, 59-96.

Vacca, R.S. (1993). Student Discipline. In *The Principal's Legal Handbook*. Topeka, KS: National Organization on Legal Problems of Education, 29-36.

Walling, D. (1995). Civic Disengagement and the Attack on Public Education. In D. Walling (Ed.), *At the Threshold of the Millenium*. Bloomington, IN: Phi Delta Kappa Educational Foundation, 33-42.

Wallis, J. (1996). *Who Speaks for God?* New York: Delacorte Press.

Wanat, C.L., Helms, L., & Engvall, R. (1994, September). Parents Versus Teachers: Avoiding Litigation in an Era of Greater Community Involvement. *People and Education*, 2(3), 320-337.

Wattenberg, B.J. (1995). *Values Matter Most*. New York: The Free Press.

Weimer, Maryellen (1993). *Improving Your Classroom Teaching*. Newbury Park, CA: Sage.

References

Weiss, C.H. (1995, Winter). The Four I's of School Reform: How Interests, Ideology, Information, and Institution Affect Teachers and Principals. *Harvard Educational Review*, 65(4), 571-592.

Weissbourd, R. (1996). *The Vulnerable Child*. Reading, MA: Addison-Wesley.

West, D.J., & Farrington, D.P. (1973). *Who Becomes Delinquent?* London, United Kingdom: Heinemann Educational Books.

Wildavsky, A. (1988). "President Reagan as a Political Strategist." In C.O. Jones (Ed.), *The Reagan Legacy: Promise and Performance*. Chatham, NJ: Chatham House, 289-305.

Willie, C.V., & Miller, I. (1988). *Social Goals and Educational Reform*. New York: Greenwood Press.

Wilson, J.Q. (1993). *The Moral Sense*. New York: The Free Press.

Wright, J.D., & Sheley, J.F. (1995). Society Should Reduce Young People's Need for Guns. In D. Bender & B. Leone (Eds.). *Crime and Criminals: Opposing Viewpoints*. San Diego, CA: Greenhaven Press, 186-193.

Index of Names

A

B

H

M

N

O

T

Tarter, C.J., 123
Thomas, Clarence, 34-35
Thomas, L.M., 122
Tucker, Marc, 142

V

Vacca, Richard S., 130, 131, 132
Vonnegut, Kurt, 7

W

Walling, Donovan, 25
Wallis, Jim, 92, 93
Wanat, Carolyn, 149
Wattenberg, Ben, 86
Webster, Noah, 46
Weimer, Maryellen, 45, 138
Weir, Margaret,43
Weiss, Carol H., 32
Weissbourd, R., 33
West, Donald James, 46, 141
Wildavsky, Aaron, 103, 104
Willie, Charles, 51, 52, 164
Willis, Bruce, 31
Wilson, James Q., 12, 18, 163
Wright, James D., 124, 125, 132

Z

Zager, Robert, 49, 51, 53, 55, 57, 58, 142, 145, 162

About the Author

Robert P. Engvall is an assistant professor of criminal justice at Mt. Mercy College in Cedar Rapids, Iowa. He holds J.D. and Ph.D. degrees from the University of Iowa, and his research interests include school law, educational and legal system "reform," collective bargaining, and "professionalism."

In addition to this book, he is the author of *The Professionalization of Teaching: Is It Truly Much Ado about Nothing?* (University Press of America, 1997). His articles have appeared in *People and Education*, *The Journal of Collective Negotiations in the Public Sector*, the *Journal of Teacher Education*, and the *Urban Review*.